Jesus Saves!
Moses Invests!

- Money
- Motivation
- Management

Victor J. Schober

Vic Schober

ISBN: 0996101047
ISBN-13: 978-0996101042

TABLE OF CONTENTS

Acknowledgements
Foreword
Preface
Introduction

Vic Schober

Acknowledgements

Many years ago I memorized a few lines from William Shakespeare's Julius Caesar that has often spoken to me. 'There is a tide in the affairs of men which, taken at the flood, leads on to fortune; omitted, all the voyage of their lives is bound in shallows and in miseries.'

He is referring to accepting or rejecting opportunity! Some have said that 'Opportunity knocks but once.' I am not sure that is completely true . . . because I have known opportunity to have knocked twice. But the point is this: When your wave comes, if you will 'hang ten' on your surf board and keep your balance, you just might be able to ride the tide all the way to the shore of success.

I want to acknowledge two of my companions in this venture called Life. First, I want to eagerly and consistently acknowledge my Lord Jesus Christ who as my best friend has shared many ventures and adventures with me. His wisdom has guided me into many arenas of fruitfulness, productivity, and good success. Thank you, Lord, for all that you have done for me and through me to the glory of our Heavenly Father!

Second, I want to acknowledge my other precious partner, my lovely wife, Naomi. We have shared so many experiences together in our over fifty-five years of marriage. She is my closest friend other than my Lord! Naomi and I have both enjoyed and endured many interesting and challenging experiences together: we are both cancer survivors; we are both credentialed ministers in the Assemblies of God in which we have been leaders in many different ministries; and we are both the parents of two wonderful children, twelve terrific grandchildren, and thus far four beautiful great-grandchildren. "Thank you, Naomi, for your love, your encouragement, your faithfulness, and your consistent faith in our Lord and in my leadership as your husband. You are the best!

We three, the Lord, Naomi and I, have often caught the 'crest of the wave' and have had the 'ride of our lives on the advancing tide' that has provided us success beyond anything we could have imagined in our early years of marriage. And it's still happening! God is good!

Jesus Saves! Moses Invests!

Forward

In the middle of the spring, 2015, I participated in a very interesting and informative seminar taught by a father and son duo, Larry Stockstill and Joel Stockstill. These inspiring men are well-known ministers connected with the Bethany Church in Baker, a suburb of Baton Rouge, Louisiana. Thank you, Larry, for speaking into my life!

Toward the end of our third day of sessions Pastor Larry taught for awhile on one way that he constructs his presentations. He cited four words to describe his approach to developing his message: Hook, Book, Look, and Took.

- The 'Hook' is the opening story that is designed to grab the attention of the audience. It needs to be one that stirs the imagination of the listener.
- The 'Book' is a reference to the Biblical scripture or story that is introduced to the audience.
- The 'Look' is referring to various illustrations from present-day life that shows clearly the truth being taught.
- The 'Took' is the one truth that each listener should take with him or her when they walk out the door of the auditorium.

I found this a very unique four point outline and made

note of it for future consideration.

Our concluding session was almost finished when I asked our moderator if I might share an experience that I had many years ago. Because my experience fit the topic we were considering at that time, I felt it would be appropriate. So, I told about the bumper sticker: 'Jesus Saves!' 'Moses Invests!'

Larry Stockstill looked intently at me, pointed his finger directly at me, and firmly said, "That's the Hook!" I knew immediately what he meant.

Earlier he had spoken prophetically over me several Spirit-led thoughts; one of which was a declaration that I would soon write a book. Well, this is that book! I was not at all considering writing another book at that time, but suddenly I was 'captured' by the idea.

I want to thank my new friend, Larry, for allowing the Holy Spirit to challenge me to begin this project which is now a 'finished project' and you hold it in your hands!

Preface

'Jesus Saves! Moses Invests!' are certainly two shocking sentences side by side, aren't they? When I first saw them presented as they are, I was confounded and conflicted, as I explain more fully in chapter one. But out of this confusion I came to more clarity on just what the Lord wanted me to know about savings and investments in several areas of my life including my finances.

In the various chapters of this book I have attempted to cover a number of topics that can occur in one's life in reference to properly managing finances, possessions, positions, profits, and a host of other things that come our way when we 'buy up opportunities' as they are presented to us.

I have learned through many years of living in good times and bad times, 'up' times and 'down' times that there is more to life than gathering an abundance of things in what the advertisers like to call the 'good life that you deserve.'

I have been greatly blessed to have all that I need plus the extras . . . as the parable says 'enough and to spare.' It is the 'spare' that I talk about in this book. What to do with the 'extras' that I have been allowed to possess!

Investing is a grand topic! It envisions planting and reaping a greater harvest! Abundance! More of everything! It promotes excitement in seeing little become much! Who doesn't thrill to having greater success with every investment?

But as this happens, there are questions that arise. Questions like: What will I do with this surplus? How will I spend it or save it or invest it? Who should I trust to help me manage it? And a multitude of other considerations!

Please know that this book is not an exhaustive study or even an attempt to share advice in the area of investments, but rather an agreement with the Lord that I would give my life full-time to the ministry of the Gospel, if He would help me to financially prosper enough to have a sufficient retirement in my latter years. We both have kept the terms of our agreement. My Lord is the best counselor-partner that anybody could ever have in this life and in the life to come!

Introduction

Perhaps some of you may wonder what credentials I have acquired that make me think I have something to say of worth and value. What experiences in my lifetime qualify me to write a book about money, motivation, and management?

If you are one of those people with such questions, I don't blame you for asking them. If you are planning to spend several hours reading the chapters of this book, you have every right to concern yourself with who I am and what I have done.

I am not the son of an investment banker or a real estate tycoon or a wealth management attorney. I am the son of a used car dealer. I am an ordained minister who has been the pastor of local congregations most of my ministry. However I have filled several administrative positions with my denomination over the past twenty years that have provided me with many management experiences. But I do not have a degree in business or finance from some Ivy League university.

I am a wealthy man when compared to most people in the many nations of the world; but when compared to the elite of our nation and successful entrepreneurs, I am simply a blessed middle-class investor who has done well following the guidance of my partner-counselor, the Lord Jesus Christ.

The stories that you will read are all true. The wisdom that you will acquire is wisdom that I acquired through reading and through personal experience as the Lord gave me direction. I have learned that experience is a great teacher. Although some of my experiences brought me pain . . . and those lessons were very well learned . . . most of my investments have been successful. I don't spend any time in this book discussing the stock market. My personal ventures in investing in it were mostly non-productive in the long run. A few such investments were okay, but the others that weren't caused me to basically 'break even'. So, that's all I will say about the stock market.

Otherwise, I think you will find this book an 'easy read'. There are plenty of interesting stories that I hope will keep you reading. Many of the chapter titles were inspired by the Spirit. After writing down a chapter title or two, I would proceed to write the body of the chapter adding illustrations that painted word pictures to hopefully make for more enjoyment on your part.

Thank you for considering this book enticing enough for you to take it and read it. May you benefit from it in many ways! Whatever you gain I pray will enrich your journey and cause you to be abundantly blessed by our generous and gracious God.

JESUS SAVES! MOSES INVESTS!

I live in Austin, Texas, the city that has unofficially adopted this motto: 'Keep Austin Weird.' Basically that means that there are many who feel perfectly at liberty to display strange and unusual bumper stickers that challenge the thoughts and the feelings of many others.

I will never forget the day that I was driving west on Northland Drive toward Loop One, commonly called MoPac Freeway by the locals because it runs parallel to the Missouri Pacific railway, when while I was waiting at the traffic light, I read this bumper sticker on the car in front of mine: 'Jesus Saves! Moses Invests!'

I was shocked! What does that mean? I read it again . . . and then once more before the light changed from red to green and that car sped away. I didn't know whether to be angry or to be perplexed. So, I think I became both.

As I drove up onto MoPac heading north toward my home, I continued to consider this unusual statement. What on earth could it be promoting? Was it meant to be anti-Christian? Was it meant to be pro-Jewish?   I was bewildered.

Slowly, but surely, I agreed with part of the slogan: 'Jesus Saves!' Yes, I do believe that Jesus Christ is the Savior. Yes, I do have faith that He saves people from their sins, if they confess those sins and then profess Christ Jesus as the Lord of their lives.

And I think I understood the other part of the slogan: 'Moses Invests!' particularly if I considered that many Jewish people know how to profitably invest their finances and prosper; so, I decided to accept that part of the bumper sticker, too. But the two statements side by side still ruffled my spirit!

It was sometime later that day that I believe the Lord allowed me to come to a personal conclusion about this

1

incident. He took this bumper sticker message and helped me to consider that it was definitely okay for me to save money in a savings account that would gain me interest; but I should also find opportunities where I could invest some of my finances and possibly gain more than what my savings account could accrue.

Still perplexed by the phrase 'Jesus Saves! Moses Invests!' I now believed that the Holy Spirit was using this unique statement to urge me to increase my meager finances both through placing some of them in a savings account and also to seek wise opportunities for investments. Yes, I now gained some peace and purpose for my financial future . . . strange as that may seem. You know God can use various mediums to relate truth to His people: the Scriptures, of course, but also sermons, songs, personal messages, and even a bumper sticker.

Much of this chapter and the other chapters in this book will focus on how to wisely use what the finances that you have accumulated beyond your needs for your monthly budgeted items that provides for food, lodging, transportation, clothing, and so forth. There is no doubt about it . . . it takes money to be born; it takes money to be buried; and it takes money to live. Someone said long ago: 'Money may not be the most important thing in life; but it sure runs a close second.' So, let's learn to be wise stewards of it!

I definitely believe that the Lord admonishes us to be wise in the use of our finances. There are more than 2,000 verses in the Bible that teach us about finances. As you continue to read this book I will refer to a number of them as I share my personal experiences as well as sharing many other stories that I have collected through the years.

AN INVESTMENT THAT RESULTED IN ANOTHER PROFITABLE INVESTMENT

As the senior pastor of the Church of Glad Tidings, Austin, I was leading our growing congregation in a fund raising program to finance a construction venture to add another building to our facilities. I knew that to be the leader I had to be out in front leading; so, after consultation with the Lord through prayer, I believed the Lord had spoken to me to pledge $10,000 to the project.

This was in 1980 when ten thousand dollars was a lot of money; and for me it was a huge amount because we did not have it. Pledging that amount of money was strictly an act of faith in God to provide it!

Less than a week after making that commitment to the Lord and to the church, a married couple from the congregation asked Naomi and me to join with them for lunch following the morning worship service that Sunday.

At lunch Eldred and Gladys Morris shared with us their desire to leave Austin and move to Dallas to become students at Christ for the Nations Institute. The Morris's were not a young couple in their twenties; they were in their mid-forties. For them this was a major move. They would have to quit their jobs, sell their home, and open a challenging chapter in their lives in another city. Eldred was a butcher in a local meat market and Gladys was a real estate agent. Big change for them!

We talked for quite awhile about all that this move would entail and then Gladys said, "I own two duplexes and I want to sell them to help finance our two years at CFNI. Could you pray with us about the sale of those duplexes?" Of course, we agreed to join with them in prayer.

That was Sunday. Then came Monday, Tuesday, and Wednesday . . . and every day I thought about those duplexes. I couldn't get them off my mind. So, Wednesday I called Gladys and said, "I just cannot get your duplexes off my mind. I think the Lord wants me to see them so that I can be better prepared to help you find someone to buy them." So, we agreed to meet the next day and take a look at them.

On Thursday we drove to north Austin and looked at

the duplex on Stobaugh. It was all brick and looked nice. This duplex had two garages. Then we drove into south Austin and looked at the duplex on James Casey. It, too, was all brick and looked nice, though it did not have a garage. It was on a street that was not connected to a major road, but could be accessed easily, if you knew how to get there.

Sitting in Gladys' car I asked her what she was asking for them. She said that she wanted to sell both of them together and that her sales price was an hundred and ten thousand dollars. She believed the north duplex was worth $65,000 and the south duplex was worth $45,000. She said that she could finance the sale herself, but that she would have to have $10,000 for the down payment.

I then approached the topic with this question: "Gladys, would you consider selling one of these duplexes to me for $3,000 down? I have just paid off my car, but I know that I can borrow three thousand dollars against it and be able to make the down payment." I continued talking with her and sharing with her my ten thousand dollar commitment to the building program and how I wondered if maybe by buying one duplex that I could manage it as rental property and then three years in the future sell it for more than the purchase price and give it to the church; whatever that gain might be. What did she think of my logic? Was it a good move? Would the property gain value in three years? Would she be willing to work with me?

She sat there silent, thinking about what I had proposed. It must have been two long minutes or more before she responded. I really thought that I had offended her. I almost broke the silence by apologizing for putting her in an awkward position. But then she spoke.

She said, "I think I will sell you both duplexes for three thousand dollars down."

I was shocked. I was elated. I was flabbergasted.

I remember saying, "Okay. I'll go to the bank

tomorrow and borrow against my car and get the down payment."

To which she retorted, "Do you know how much interest the bank will charge you?" Remember that in 1980 we were under the Jimmy Carter administration in Washington, D. C. and our national financial picture was a mess.

I answered, "I think I'll probably have to pay nineteen or twenty percent interest."

Gladys responded, "Yes, and that is robbery! It's terrible! No, you must not go to the bank; I will loan you that down payment of three thousand dollars for ten percent interest."

There it was! I would soon be the owner of two duplexes for essentially no money down. Oh, there would be a loan of three thousand dollars to be paid off in five years, plus the loan for one hundred and seven thousand dollars that would be on a fifteen year note payable to Gladys. How could anything be better than that?

So, within weeks I was the owner of investment property to pay for a greater investment . . . in the Kingdom of God! My Lord was my partner and we were in business together for better or worse, for richer or poorer.

Well, God doesn't make mistakes!

To summarize the outcome of this investment venture in real estate I will simply say that I was able to pay my pledge to the Church of Glad Tidings in less than three years. Interestingly it was made possible through another investment that the Lord engineered.

I did not sell those two duplexes for many years. In the meantime the duplex on James Casey became quite valuable when the South Austin Medical Center was built immediately adjacent to my property. After being approached by the hospital through a realtor for several years I finally decided to sell it to them for a lot more than I had purchased it from Gladys. With the proceeds from that sale I purchased two more duplexes in Austin and a small apartment house complex, too.

I owned the north Austin duplex for many years and finally sold it a few years ago for a big profit. What can I say . . . I really now believe that 'Jesus Saves . . . and Jesus Invests!'

You may find this as an interesting side note: the small apartment house complex was a block from the former Mueller Airport in Austin which was once the major airport for the city before the Austin Bergstrom International Airport was opened. Yes, once again another hospital was built not far from my property . . . the Dell Children's Medical Center just off Interstate 35 and 51st Street. No, I did not know of either hospital having plans to build where they built, but God knew it. He really is a great partner to have when you are investing!

This was the beginning! God opened my eyes to other opportunities in real estate investment through the years. I also learned that it is important to have a savings account because there are times when there is a need for immediate access to funds, so having some liquidity is necessary. But I discovered that buying investment properties is even more important.

I may mention some of those investments later in this book to illustrate other truths that I have learned along the way. God is good! God is wise! God loves to bless His children!

Investments usually require patience on our part. Rarely does an investment yield immediate gains. Occasionally an investment will pay quick dividends, but most of the time we are required to be patient and wait . . . sometimes for years before reaping a handsome return.

I heard a friend of mine say recently that in our society these days people are so impatient that while sitting in their cars as they are slowly advancing in an automatic car wash, they are fuming and fussing that there should be a fast lane for people in a hurry.

There are several admonitions in the Scriptures that are appropriate here: "Be patient, brothers, see how the farmer waits for the land to yield its valuable crop and how patient he is for the autumn and spring rains. You too, be patient and stand firm." (James 5:7, 8) Jesus exhorted his followers: "In your patience possess you your souls." (Luke 21:19)

If you plant today and expect to harvest tomorrow, you will be greatly disappointed. All investments take time . . . sometimes years . . . to produce a healthy gain. So, be prepared to wait. It's usually very worth the wait.

Occasionally I hear of someone making an investment in raw land and rather quickly having someone offer to buy it from them within weeks of the purchase for a sizable profit. It does happen . . . but not often.

I know of other investors who have purchased many acres of land with the idea of selling some of the more valuable, more visible acres for what they originally paid for the entire acreage. This leaves them with possibly as many acres as they sold off, or maybe even more, debt free. But now they must wait patiently for their profit to come in a few years when they sell the remaining acres. Patience! In time the remaining acreage will gain in value, too.

I once purchased a large older house that was situated on over a half of an acre of land in the inner city of Austin. I then subdivided the house into two apartments making it a desirable duplex. It was fun watching the project develop over several months.

Oh, I learned a few things in the process. I learned that by making it a duplex the codes required me to completely rewire the electrical system and re-do the plumbing system. I was forced into investing more than I had originally intended. But thankfully it had a pier and beam foundation; so, redoing the plumbing was not as expensive as it could have been had it been built on a slab foundation.

When the project was completed, I leased out the two apartments for several years. I waited and was patient. At the right time I placed it on the realty market and made a good profit from my investment.

SILVER AND GOLD HAVE I SOME

When I mention the word 'gold', what picture comes to your mind? Gold rings and gold jewelry; or maybe a collection of gold coins; or if you are a history buff, maybe the California 'gold rush' in the mid-nineteenth century. Maybe some other picture comes to mind; hopefully it's not a misconstrued mental picture of the motto on our United States currency: 'In Gold We Trust.'

In 1980 Kevin Hillier, a resident of Australia who lived in a trailer park, purchased a new metal detector and began searching for hidden metal items. As he began searching in his backyard, he discovered something that he had never expected to find. In fact the readings on his metal detector were so abnormal that he almost didn't pick up his shovel and dig into the soil to investigate what it was. But he did! He had dug only about a foot deep in his yard when his shovel hit something solid. He continued his digging . . . and soon uncovered a large 'stone.' It was a 61 pound nugget of gold! Wow!

Kevin no longer lives in a trailer park. He eventually sold the huge rock of gold to a casino in Las Vegas, Nevada for well over a million dollars. Interestingly enough he sold it to the 'Golden Nugget' Casino many years ago.

Kevin's nugget was really big, but there have been bigger ones dug from the ground in the past. Most of them have been melted down for the gold that was in them. For example, one nugget was called the 'Matrix' and contained about 187 pounds of gold. The 'Welcome Stranger' nugget weighed in at about 148 pounds of gold. The 'Golden Eagle' was about 71 pounds heavy.

These days with gold at such high prices per ounce . . . if the owners of these nuggets had been patient, they would now be extremely wealthy individuals, extremely rich. Hopefully they kept some percentage of that gold for themselves as a long-term investment when they sold their nuggets.

To some people gold is their god. They worship their accumulated gold. They have golden gods literally! One of the first gods of ancient Israel was made of gold. It was a golden calf.

You remember the story. Moses had gone up the mountain to with meet God and was gone for forty days. As the Israelites in the valley below became impatient, they foolishly went to Aaron and said: 'Come, make us gods who will go before us. As for this fellow Moses who brought us up out of Egypt, we don't know what has happened to him.' (Exodus 32:1 NIV)

Aaron foolishly listened to their pleas. Rather than standing firm in his commitment to the living God, he instructed them to give him their golden earrings. Then he melted the gold and made an idol of the melted gold. A solid gold calf god!

Of course, Jehovah God would not stand for such idolatry. He severely rebuked them and chastised them. Moses demanded that the golden calf idol be crushed and ground into grains of golden sand and powder. Then he had the powder scattered upon the water and made the people drink it.

The very first of the Ten Commandments says: 'You shall have no other gods before me. You shall not make for yourself an idol in the form of anything in heaven above or on the earth beneath. You shall not bow down to them or worship them.' (Exodus 20:3-5 NIV)

I have been to Bangkok, Thailand, where I saw a huge idol called the Golden Buddha that is a statue that is 9.8 feet tall weighing approximately 5.4 long tons or 6.1 short tons. It can be disassembled into nine pieces. At US $1,400 per troy ounce, the gold in the statue is estimated to be worth more than $250,000,000. The body of the idol is 40% pure, the volume from the chin to the forehead is

80% pure, and the hair and the topknot, weighing 45 kg, are 99% pure gold. Buddhists from all over the world come to worship this Golden Buddha. As I stood as a tourist to see this idol in the Viharn building that had been built to house it in 1954-55, I observed many men and women bowing before it in worship.

There is an interesting story that I want to share with you concerning this statue. When the idol was being moved to its new location on May 25, 1955, it was not known that this statue was made of gold because for many, many years it had been encased in a plaster coating that had hidden the gold from being seen.

In the final attempt to lift the statue from its pedestal, the ropes broke, and the statue fell hard on the ground. At that moment, some of the plaster coating chipped off, allowing the gold surface underneath to be seen. Work was immediately stopped so that an evaluation could be made.

All the plaster was carefully removed, revealing this gold idol now known at the Golden Buddha. It is believed that it had been encased in stucco since the mid-1760s to keep it from being stolen by Burmese invaders. At the time of King Rama III (1824-1851) the statue, still covered with stucco, was installed as the principal Buddha image in the main temple building of Wat Chotanaram in Bangkok. The true identity of this idol had been forgotten for almost 200 years. What an interesting history!

In the 19th century novel by George Eliot entitled Silas Marner the old miser Silas often would remove his bag of golden coins and fingered them affectionately as if they were his friends; as if they were gods to be worshiped.

But he came to the place that he loved his child more than he loved his coins and he became a benevolent giver rather than a greedy, miserly 'getter.'

Silver and gold have held a strangle hold of avarice on many a man and woman throughout history. Many people have been murdered because of lust for silver and gold. There are many stories from history in which wars were fought for treasures of precious metals and precious jewels. One example is the story of the Spaniards who killed and robbed the Inca Indians of their silver and gold in the 1700s. Tens of thousands died due to the lust for gold.

Do people still lust for silver and gold and do unlawful things to obtain it? Yes, of course.

Do you remember the founder and president of the American Atheists Madalyn Murray O'Hair?

Since she lived for years in Austin, Texas, I became well acquainted with some of her activities. But it was only after she was murdered on September 29, 1995, that I learned much more about her and her criminal activities.

I personally know a former FBI agent (who shall remain anonymous) who told me some of the inside story of this infamous woman and her lust for gold.

She was the president of the American Atheists from 1963 to 1986 and then one of her sons, Jon Garth Murray, became the president of the organization from 1986 to 1995, while she remained de facto president during those nine years.

O'Hair is best known for the Murray v. Curlett lawsuit, which led to a landmark ruling in 1963 by the Supreme Court in Washington, D.C. which prohibited official Bible-reading in American public schools. This came just one year after the Supreme Court prohibited officially sponsored prayer in public schools in the Engel v. Vitale lawsuit.

In 1995 she was kidnapped, murdered and mutilated, along with her son Jon Garth Murray and her granddaughter Robin Murray O'Hair.

Eventually the killers were caught. They were a convicted felon named David Roland Waters, who was out of prison on parole, and two fellow career criminals Danny Fry and Gary Karr. Waters had been a member of the American Atheists from February 1993 to April 1994 and had served as the office manager for the organization. It was later learned that he had discovered a document that linked Madalyn with a secret bank account in New Zealand containing over a million dollars.

On August 27, 1995, Madalyn, Jon, and Robin suddenly disappeared. The door to the office of the American Atheists was locked with a typewritten note attached and signed presumably by Jon that read: 'The Murray O'Hair family has been called out of town on an emergency basis. We do not know how long we will be gone at the time of the writing of this memo.'

When the O'Hair home was entered later on, their breakfast dishes were on the table, her diabetes medication was on the kitchen countertop, and her dogs had been left without a caregiver. A few days later the trio called with a claim that they were on business in San Antonio. Then a few days after that, Jon ordered $600,000 worth of gold coins from a San Antonio jeweler but took delivery of only $500,000 worth of coins.

Until September 27 several of the organization's employees received telephone calls from Jon and Robin stating they were okay and that nothing was amiss. The employees would state later that they felt that their voices sounded stressed and strained. After September 28 there were no more calls.

As we now know the godless Murray-O'Hair trio were murdered and mutilated on September 29th. Or it could have been the other way around . . . mutilated and murdered . . . we don't know. All that we actually do know is that when their body parts were found buried in a shallow grave on a ranch in south Texas, it was difficult to determine who was who.

We now know that David Waters took the half-million dollars in gold coins and immediately spent about $80,000 of it in less than a week on wild, riotous partying. The other $420,000 worth of gold coins he put in a suitcase and locked it up in a storage park in north Austin.

Interestingly enough some thieves with a key that just

happened to work on the padlock Waters had placed on the door of the storage closet, stole all the gold coins and spent them all. Well, not quite all because when this band of thieves were finally apprehended there was one coin remaining, only one.

A secret bank account with over a million dollars in it in New Zealand most likely spoke of illicit funds in Madalyn Murray O'Hair's name; probably monies she had embezzled from the American Atheists funds. A half of a million dollars in gold coins spoke of more wrong doing by the crooks that they all were: a godless woman with her son and granddaughter; three killer criminals; plus a band of petty thieves who struck it rich for awhile. What a sad story! Obviously gold was their god! Madalyn Murray O'Hair died godless and goldless!

Is it wrong to have gold? Is possession of gold a sign of greed? Is gold equal to gross sin?

The answers to those three questions are simply 'No.' Gold in itself is neither good nor bad. God had Moses create special vessels for use in the Tabernacle and they were made of gold. The Bible tells us that even the streets in the New Jerusalem are of gold.

Just as the Scriptures tell us that it is not money, but the love of money that is the root of all evil. So it is true of gold. If a person is so enamored with the possession of gold that it becomes a driving desire to have more and more of it, then most likely there is idolatry involved.

Since it is okay to own some silver and gold, how much should a portfolio have?

First, let me say that silver and gold have I some. Rather than saying how much in dollar figures, I prefer to say that it is a very small percentage of my portfolio of investments. Should I have more? Possibly.

I will be quick to say that silver and gold is without doubt a safer medium than the dollar (paper money) appears to be.

Since the inception of the Federal Reserve Bank in

1913, experts tell us that the dollar has lost 97.8% of its value. In 1913 an ounce of gold was priced at $20.67. In June 2015 one ounce of gold was priced at $1190.00.

Another way of stating the decline of the value of the dollar is this:

In 1776 the dollar was worth $1.00.
In 1896 the dollar was worth $1.00.
In 1926 the dollar was worth $0.50.
In 1956 the dollar was worth $0.25.
In 2015 the dollar was worth $0.02.

One more way of visualizing the dollar's decline is to say that from 1790 until 1913 the loss of value of the dollar was about 8%. Since 1913 the dollar has lost another 95% of its value.

The Federal Reserve's mandate is to maintain price stability in our nation, but from observation of the facts it has undermined the dollar's value instead.

Obviously owning silver and gold is more preferable to owning paper dollars that continue to lose value as time marches on.

But know this, silver and gold also fluctuate in value from week to week. By the time this book goes to press it could be greater in value than it presently is or it could be lesser in value than when you purchased it, whichever way you wish to measure it.

I am not a financial advisor. I do not wish to be a financial advisor for anyone. I do own some silver and gold coins that do fluctuate in value. I have not closely followed that fluctuation because I expect it to do so over time. I actually think that for the present it is down from where it was when I made my purchases. Do I wish that it was higher? Of course! But when making an investment in precious metals, it is for the long haul. Just know that wise investors purchase silver and gold with the idea of holding that investment for years.

But allow me to finish this chapter by commenting about the title to this chapter: 'Silver and Gold Have I Some.' That is a slight 'take-off' on what the Apostle Peter said to the physically challenged man at the Gate Beautiful when he said, 'Silver and gold have I none but such as I have give I thee. In the name of Jesus Christ of Nazareth rise up and walk.' Peter and John had a very wealthy portfolio in the Spirit! Maybe they didn't have silver or gold . . . but they did have exceedingly powerful connections to the One who owned it all.

Would I consider my silver and gold coins to be of less value than the power to say to a lame man in the name of Jesus Christ rise up and walk? Absolutely! Having the authority of Christ's name to speak health into any infirm body is of much greater value . . . by far! I am confident that the crippled man would agree. He would much rather walk than have a few coins in his pocket, right?

May we who are believers in the power of the name of Jesus Christ always keep our priorities on the straight and narrow path. Silver, gold, money, and possessions of value are never, never worth more than our relationship to our Lord. May we ever properly evaluate our relationship to the Holy Spirit as of far greater value than anything that we may possess!

In comparison to what I own and what my portfolio says I am worth financially . . . I have nothing, nothing compared to my Lord's love for me. His grace and favor are among the most valuable items I have in this life here on earth and in the life to come in eternity.

Jesus said: 'Watch out! Be on your guard against all kinds of greed; a man's life does not consist in the abundance of his possessions.' (Luke 12:15 NIV)

IF IT SEEMS TOO GOOD TO BE TRUE . . . CHECK IT OUT . . . THEN MAKE YOUR DECISION

I am fully aware of the familiar saying: 'If it seems too good to be true . . . it probably is,' but I choose to acknowledge it might be true. I have had experiences that have led me to believe that there are instances where it may have seemed too good, but it was true nonetheless.

I once lived in Keller, Texas, one of several of the 'mid-cities' in the Dallas-Fort Worth metroplex, while serving as the district superintendent of the North Texas District of the Assemblies of God. I was driving all over the district from the Oklahoma border to San Marcos, from the Louisiana border to Abilene, and from Wichita Falls to Nacogdoches and all points in between. It is a really big territory including over five hundred and fifty churches and over eighteen hundred ministers.

My car was getting older and more 'experienced' every month and I decided it was time to begin searching for a newer car with much less mileage than my present vehicle. Yes, I could have purchased a brand new car, but that's not in my DNA. My upbringing in the home of my father, a used car dealer in San Antonio, taught me that purchasing a new car is the 'world's worst investment.' He had trained me to wisely search for 'an experienced automobile' that might be two to three years old and one that had been kept meticulously and was not driven too often. In other words, a car that was really clean and with low mileage.

So, I began my search on the internet. I had already owned two Lexus four-door sedans and they had been really fine transportation, so I was once again looking for another Lexus. Dad had shown me by example that owning a top of the line automobile was good business. Usually those cars were previously owned by more mature people who didn't misuse their cars, but rather maintained them well; often times having it regularly serviced at their local new car dealership.

For several weeks I had been occasionally looking on a number of websites and was becoming well educated as to the range of prices that was being asked for each year and model of car. In other words, I had been diligent in learning what was available and what it would cost me.

Then, one day as I was perusing a particular listing of cars being offered by a car dealer in Farmer's Branch, a suburb of Dallas, I noticed a three-year old Lexus that had low mileage and was said to be in excellent, like-new condition being offered for ten thousand dollars less than other similar automobiles. This really looked to be 'too good to be true.'

I decided to immediately print the page that I had just seen on my computer and then I told Naomi that I would be gone for a couple of hours to look at a Lexus that was for sale. I would give her a call later on.

When I found the dealership, I discovered that they had an indoor showroom for their used cars and that those cars really did look like new cars.

After a few minutes of looking around, I found the Lexus that I had come to see. Soon a salesman approached me, asking if he could help me. I pointed to this beautiful black Lexus LS400 sedan and asked him if the price listed on the inventory sheet taped to the back window was negotiable. He said that their policy was to ask a low price upfront and not to spend time in negotiations with their customers.

Well, that certainly was a different approach; so, I reached into my pocket and unfolded the sheet that I had printed earlier and asked him if this car was still available. He looked at the sheet, looked at the inventory sheet taped to the back window, and then he carefully looked at the two again, checking the inventory numbers, and finally he said that he would need to go talk with the owner.

I watched as they conversed, looking at the sheet I had given to the salesman, and they talked some more . . . then slowly the owner himself came over to talk with me.

The bottom line was this: his son had made a typographical error when entering the information on his computer! I had the proof of a ten thousand dollar error! The owner knew he had to honor his advertising or face a possible law suit, so he simply said, "You've got me. I guess I'll have to sell you this car for much less than what I have in it. You've sure got yourself a super deal!"

Within an hour or so I was driving my new acquisition (almost like new) Lexus back to Keller . . . about as happy as a used car buyer could ever be who had just made a fabulous $10,000 savings on the purchase of a really nice auto!

Was it 'too good to be true'? In nine out ten cases (or maybe 99 out of 100 cases) it would have been simply too good to be true, but not in this case. I was a blessed man!

What if I had not checked it out? What if I had said: 'This is really too good to be true!' What if I had said: 'This has got to be some kind of a 'bait and switch' trick?

I have purchased many used cars in my life, but never have I done this well! I had bought a beautiful vehicle for $20,000 that was worth $30,000! I usually speak better English than this, but 'Ain't God good?'

Why was I the one who was so blessed? I truly believe that it was the Lord giving back to me in an unusual way finances that I had been giving to Him in offerings for various missions' ventures, church-related projects, and so forth. Taking God as your business partner is simply good business. Investments in His Kingdom pay great dividends . . . and those dividends can come in really unique ways.

Have I always recognized those dividends? I must confess that I have not always done so.

Naomi and I had moved back to the Austin area in 2008 to a neighborhood of homes in Williamson County between Round Rock and Cedar Park . . . in the Brushy Creek area . . . and I had just become acquainted with our neighbors. One neighbor had actually attended the Church of Glad Tidings in Austin for a few months where I had served as the senior pastor for over twenty-seven years. Meeting him after moving in was a very pleasant surprise.

You will remember that within months America experienced the financial crash that we now call the Great Recession and many people would lose lots of money as the stock market plunged downward. Others would lose their jobs. Some would have to take bankruptcy. Many would have to allow their homes to be foreclosed upon by their bank or mortgage company. It was really a perilous time for people all over America.

My neighbor was a real estate agent who was struggling to make it happen in such difficult times. People were afraid to make any major purchases because they didn't know what was going to happen next. The future looked dark and dismal.

After months of little or no sales, my neighbor told me that he had no choice but to take bankruptcy, even though he hated the very thought of doing so.

He then told me: 'Pastor, I'll give you my house. All you have to do is pick up the monthly payments. We are moving to Houston and I hope to find work there.'

I walked through his house observing what it was like. It had a beautiful backyard with a swimming pool. It had many large trees on about an acre of land that was on the banks of a medium sized spring-fed pond/lake. The house was a brick home of approximately 2400 square feet of floor space. It was in need of a number of upgrades, but basically a good investment for no money down, just pick up the payments.

It was mine for the taking, but I failed to see the future with eyes of faith. I allowed the negative financial problems in the nation to overwhelm me, even though Central Texas was not being hit as hard as most other areas of the country.

After thinking about his offer for a few days, I expressed to him my gratitude for his offer and I told him that had decided not to accept it.

But knowing what I now know, I should have graciously accepted his offer, leased it out to someone even if I had to take a slight loss on the monthly payments. After all . . . I would not have had any investment initially in making the purchase.

Within three years I could have sold the house and made twenty thousand dollars; within five years I could have sold the house and made over fifty thousand dollars; but I didn't . . . because it seemed too good to be true. People don't just give you a house . . . or do they? Have I regretted my decision? Of course, wouldn't you?

Oh, I have had a couple of other experiences that really were 'too good to be true' . . . like the time I was contacted about committing to take a two-hour tour of a 'time-share like offer' at the Horseshoe Bay Resort near Marble Falls, Texas, on Lake LBJ. Earlier I had driven through the beautiful neighborhoods in Horseshoe Bay and had thought what a great place to have a vacation. There are two beautifully landscaped golf courses, plus access to a wonderful lake for skiing, fishing, or boating. So, when I got this offer, I decided to give it a second thought.

They were promising one of three enticing gifts just for coming out and taking the tour . . . even if you didn't buy into their program. All three gifts sounded too good to be true, but they said unequivocally that one of those gifts would be given. I particularly remember that one of the gifts was a boat.

In my mind's eye I could see a canoe or a kayak or a small fishing boat for two. What else could 'a boat' mean?

Well, to get to the point I am making, when we had finished the two hour tour and went back to their office, they lived up to their promise. I was given 'a boat'! It fit into a cardboard box that I carried out to my car and put in the trunk. It was an inflatable plastic boat-shaped float for one child to use at a swimming pool, but it was 'a boat.' It was too good to be true!

I remember another time when I really thought it was a good thing! I actually paid an hundred dollars for a two-night stay in one of three well-known hotels in San Antonio plus a lovely dinner for two on the San Antonio Riverwalk in a restaurant that I knew was an excellent place for dinner.

We chose the St. Anthony Hotel which was famous for its beautiful lobby and the gorgeous chandeliers that were in it.

So I took Naomi there to celebrate our wedding anniversary in June. Everything seemed to be A-OK . . . until we got off the elevator on the floor where our room was located.

Although the St. Anthony Hotel had been going through a major remodeling project to upgrade it to be once again a great hotel . . . this particular floor had not been remodeled for a long time. Our room was small, unattractive, needing a lot of things redone, and the bathroom looked like it was an hundred years old. I can't begin to adequately describe our shock at what we saw and where we were planning to stay for two nights.

The bottom line again was major disappointment! We did stay one night, but checked out early the next morning, never to return. Oh, the dinner was fine though. What else can I say? Watch out for major promotional gimmicks by hustlers purporting to really want you to have a super good deal because 'you deserve it.' I've had a couple of those . . . and I guess because of my stupidity in allowing myself to get caught in their trap, I did 'deserve it.'

Experience is a great teacher! I think that I have learned my lesson . . . I think. My German father once had an interesting sign in the office at his used car lot in San

Antonio: 'We get so soon oldt and so late schmart!'

Maybe by the time we live to be 100 years old we'll 'know it all' . . . but by then it's too late, huh?

Oh, by the way, I read recently that right now there are over 100,000 people in America who are over 100 years old. That's a lot of collective wisdom! Hopefully they are wise enough not to get trapped in some 'get rich quick scheme.' But if not, please help them to refrain!

It amazes me the vast number of older and younger people, too, who collectively spend millions of dollars on the Lotto and similar gimmicks. As someone said: 'The lottery is simply a tax on people who are bad at math.'

MONEY MATTERS . . . MORE OR LESS

I am a native born citizen of the United States of America. I am a native born Texan having been born in San Antonio, Texas. I presently live in Williamson County just north of Austin, Texas. I am officially a retired senior pastor; however, I do presently have three part time jobs which include serving the Church of Glad Tidings, Austin, as the leader of the OASIS Ministry (Older Adults Serving, Interacting, Sharing); serving my district as the Regional Executive Presbyter of the South Central Region; and serving as an interim pastor for the Calvary Worship Center, Austin. All three of these positions provide a part time salary.

So, though I am considered to be a retiree, I am quite busy serving in three part time positions.

Understand that I would not be doing this if I didn't fully enjoy being active and busy in the work of the Kingdom of God. I stay busy and I stay happy and it's not because of the money.

I say all of that to give you a quick look at my present life because it sets the stage for what I now want to share with you.

I recently learned of a web site that compares American incomes to the world's incomes. That Web address is http://givingwhatwecan.org/why-give/how-rich-am-I. I was curious. So I used this site to compare my income with that of the rest of the world. When I plugged in the numbers of my part time salaries, I learned that I am considered to be in the top 2% of the world's richest individuals. I was shocked!

This program indicated that my monthly income from my three part time jobs plus my monthly retirement account check makes my intake to be 32 times more than the global average. That, too, was very shocking!

In my lifetime I have traveled extensively in over forty nations of the world. I have visited and seen a lot of cities and towns and villages and the way some people live. I have seen many shanty towns populated by very poor families. I have ministered in villages where there was no running water or adequate sewage. I have traveled to places where people lived in make shift cardboard and plywood one room shacks.

I have also visited and ministered in beautiful cities and places where we stayed in lovely hotels and ate wonderful meals. We have toured museums, palaces, churches, and parks that were well kept and beautifully landscaped. There were places in the Caribbean, in Europe, and in South America that were so nice, so pleasant that I would love to visit there again.

What I am attempting to convey is this: I am not naïve or uneducated. I have seen some of the worst places and some of the best places in the world, but when I typed in my numbers and then read how I compared to the average person in the world to buying things that I need to survive, I was stunned.

Without doubt I am a very blessed, rich person. The chances are that you are, too!

But to further expand on this thought read this. It is a fact that a family of two in America making $15,500 a year (that's poverty level) is still in the top 18% of the world's richest people. A family of two at poverty level in our nation makes almost 6 times as much as the average person in the world to buy things they need to survive. We Americans (the vast majority of us) are extremely wealthy compared to the rest of the world.

Now what? This is not just a guess but a fact that you are rich, what does that mean to you? Is that good or bad? If you are a born again, Bible believing Christian, what does God's Word say about this topic?

Before I answer that question, have you lived long enough to know the name Jack Benny? He was once a comedian in the early days of television when he entertained people all across the nation with his wit and winsome stories. He once said that a thief pointed a gun at him and said: 'Your money or your life.' After a long pause, Benny said, 'I'm thinking. I'm thinking.' The question for Benny was: Does money matter more or less?

When we think of really wealthy people in America's history, we think of John D. Rockefeller, who once said: 'I've made many millions but they brought me no real happiness. I'd barter them all for the days when I sat on an office stool in Cleveland and counted myself rich on $3.00 a week.'

Or W. H. Vanderbilt who said: 'The care of my hundreds of millions is too great a load for any brain or back to bear. It's enough to kill anyone. There's no pleasure left in it.' It was John Jacob Astor who spent his life as a victim of ulcers and depression, who said: 'I'm the most miserable man on earth.' Andrew Carnegie noted that 'millionaires seldom ever smile.'

Sylvester Stallone was asked several years ago about what effect money had on his life. He answered: 'Money does not bring peace of mind. Actually it brings more problems. Everything is magnified one hundred thousand times. That's not to complain. But once you make a fortune, you'd think it would be all green lights and blue skies. But that's not true. As a matter of fact it brings out some of the most vile characteristics that you can imagine.'

Even though these well known wealthy tycoons and Stallone decry the pain and burden of having too much money, I heard of a guy wearing a T-shirt recently that exhibited this prayer: 'Lord, let me prove that winning the Lotto won't ruin me.'

Okay, you may have millions of dollars in your investment portfolio or you may still be working hard on your first million, but please pay attention to this piece of advice: 'Command those who are rich in this present world not to be arrogant nor to put their hope in wealth, which is so uncertain, but to put their hope in God, who richly provides us with everything for our enjoyment. Command them to do good, to be rich in good deeds, and to be generous and willing (ready) to share. In this way they will lay up treasure for themselves as a firm foundation for the coming age, so that they may take hold of the life that is truly life.' Paul wrote this advice to his spiritual son Timothy in his first epistle to him in chapter six verses seventeen through nineteen.'

Let me share a simple outline from an article written by John Sears from the advice Paul gave Timothy. Sears entitled this article 'How to Handle Wealth.'

1. God provided it; don't be arrogant.
2. God provided it; be thankful.
3. God provided it; have a community spirit.

The Apostle Paul did not condemn people for being wealthy. But he did give those of us who are wealthy by the world's standards wisdom about how to properly handle our wealth. He offers to us the best investment plan available for a long term gain on our money. Read it again: 'Be rich in good deeds . . . be generous and willing to share your wealth . . . lay up treasure for the coming age. Take hold of the life that is truly life!' Invest in your future! Money matters more that way! Without that kind of investment plan money matters much less!

Someone has written this piece of wisdom. I liked it so I share it here:

- Money can buy a bed but it cannot buy sleep,
- Money can buy amusements but it cannot buy happiness,
- Money can buy companions but it cannot buy friends,
- Money can buy books but it cannot buy brains,
- Money can buy a house but it cannot buy a

home,
- Money can buy medicine but it cannot buy health,
- Money can buy flattery but it cannot buy respect.

But money invested as Paul exhorted Timothy can buy 'life that is truly life.'

Does money matter more or less with Jesus and with God?

Here are the facts:

- Sixteen of the 38 parables in the Scriptures are concerned with how to handle money and possessions.
- In the Gospels an amazing one out of 10 verses deal directly with the subject of money.
- The Bible offers more than 500 verses on prayer, less than 500 verses on faith, but more than 2000 verses on money and possessions.

We all know that it takes money to live, to eat, to be clothed, to maintain a home, to have transportation, and many other necessities like insurance and education. This chapter is not minimizing the role of money in our lives, but rather maximizing the proper perspective that we must maintain in our relationship with money, finances, and investments.

We have talked some about savings and investments. What does Jesus teach about them?

In Matthew 25 which is about the End Times Jesus tells this story: 'A man going on a journey called his servants and entrusted his property to them. To one he gave five talents of money, to another two talents, and to another one talent, each according to his ability. Then he went on his journey.

The man who had received the five talents went at once and put his money to work and gained five more. So also the one with two talents gained two more. But the man who had received the one talent went off, dug a hole in the ground and hid his master's money.

After a long time the master of those servants returned and settled accounts with them. The man who had received the five talents brought the other five. 'Master' he said, 'you entrusted me with five talents. See, I have gained five more.'

His master replied, 'Well done, good and faithful servant! You have been faithful with a few things, I will put you in charge of many things. Come and share your master's happiness!'

The man with the two talents also came. 'Master' he said, 'you entrusted me with two talents; see, I have gained two more.' His master replied, 'Well done, good and faithful servant! You have been faithful with a few things; I will put you in charge of many things. Come and share your master's happiness!'

Then the man who had received the one talent came. 'Master' he said, 'I knew that you are a hard man, harvesting where you have not sown and gathering where you have not scattered seed. So I was afraid and went out and hid your talent in the ground. See, here is what belongs to you.'

His master replied, 'You wicked, lazy servant! So you knew that I harvest where I have not sown and gather where I have not scattered seed? Well then, you should have put my money on deposit with the bankers, so that when I returned I would have received it back with interest.'

Take the talent from him and give it to the one who has the ten talents. For everyone who has will be given more and he will have abundance. Whoever does not have, even what he has will be taken from him.'

There are many things we can learn from this powerful parable. Here are seven of them:

1. What we have is not ours. (v. 14)
2. We're given what we can handle. (v. 15)
3. We must invest what we've been given. (v.16, 18)
4. A day of accountability is coming. (v. 19)
5. What we do with what we have reveals our view of God. (v. 20-25)
6. What we have we must use or what we have we will lose. (v.26)
7. Who you know and what you do will lead to either abundance or agony. (v. 26)

These are important observations but I want to focus on two things that are pertinent to our subject matter: Jesus commends two men who have made successful investments. He believes in investing! Jesus condemns the man who does not invest his money, but he tells him he should have at least put it in a savings account at the bank.

He encourages both having investments and having a savings account, but he seems much more pleased with the practice of investing. He congratulates the investors, calling them 'good and faithful' men. Then beyond that he rewards them with major promotions!

It cannot be more plainly stated that in the field of finances our Lord was an astute businessman. He explains to all who are listening that fruitful, profitable stewards will actually receive much more for diligently working with their portfolio. But if you are fearful and lazy, you will lose everything that you have had placed within your portfolio. See this: at the very least you might escape the master's wrath if you put it in a savings' account for a little gain of interest.

Money Matters . . . More or Less! Don't be fearful or frivolous with your money! Watch where others are wisely investing and do the same . . . don't put your money in an envelope or shoe box and gain nothing. Until you make your investment, place your money where you can receive the most interest on your savings. I suggest you check with the North Texas District of the Assemblies of God where at present (2015) you will receive 3% interest on a one year certificate of deposit with their program. I know of no other place where you will gain more annually.

The more I read the teachings of my Lord, the more I strongly believe that the bumper sticker I saw years ago that said: 'Jesus Saves! Moses invests!' has it only partially correct. I now believe that 'Jesus Saves! Jesus Invests!' is so much more correct.

'AT WHAT PRICE' ADVICE

Everything has its price! Rarely does anything come without cost! Occasionally you may receive something free, but not often. Usually there is a price tag attached, whether you see it or not. Learn to be more discerning about 'hidden costs' that will eventually zap you sometimes by surprise; particularly if you blindly assume all is what it seems to be.

DEBT . . . 'Till debt do us part'

If you were to have a discussion with any marriage counselor, asking him or her about what kind of problems bring on separation and divorce, among the many reasons they may mention it is certain that financial debt is one of them.

They may mention problems with in-laws (and outlaws). They may mention incompatibility between the two marriage partners. Some have defined this to mean: (1) not enough income and (2) not enough 'pat-ability' meaning caressing. Some say the lack of loving communication.

But it is for sure that the weight of heavy debt due to overburdened credit cards, buying too much house for too little income, and so forth definitely contributes to 'Till debt do us part' or divorce.

'The rich rule over the poor, and the borrower is servant to the lender.' (Proverbs 22:7)

'A creditor may seize all he has; strangers may plunder the fruits of his labor.' (Psalm 109:11)

'To which of my creditors did I sell you? Because of your sins you were sold.' (Isaiah 50:1)

GREED . . . 'Be freed from greed!'

Have you heard the story of John G. Wendell and his sisters? Even though they had received a huge inheritance from their parents, they were some of the most miserly people you can imagine. They spent very little of their wealth and did all that they could to keep it for themselves.

John was able to influence five of his six sisters to never marry, but for all of them to live in the same house in New York City for fifty years. When the last sister died in 1931, the estate was valued at over $1,000,000! She had one dress to her name and had worn it for over twenty-five years.

The Wendell family had such a compulsion to greedily hold on to their money and possessions that they lived like paupers. They were the embodiment of people who Jesus described as a fool 'who lays up treasure for himself, and is not rich toward God.' (Luke 12:21)

Or have you heard of Bertha Adams? She died in 1976 at the age of 71 in Palm Beach, Florida. The coroner's report said that she died of malnutrition, weighing only 50 pounds. She had often begged for food. Her house was like 'a pig-pen' . . . excessively filthy.

Many thought that she was extremely poor. But two keys were found to two safety deposit boxes: in one box there was over 700 shares of AT&T stock and approximately $200,000 in cash and in the second box there was over $600,000 in cash. What an example of a greed-filled, hoarding fool!

Have you heard of the 'Toddler's Creed'?

If I want it, it's mine.
If I gave it to you and change my mind later, it's mine.
If I can take it away from you, it's mine.
If I had it a little while ago, it's mine.
If it's mine, it will never belong to you or anyone else, no matter what.

If we are building something together, all the pieces are mine.

If it looks just like mine, it is mine.

(Elisa Morgan, president of MOPS – International 'Mothers Of Pre-Schoolers.')

Sometimes toddlers who grow up to be adults never grow out of this stage of thinking; they believe that all their things belong to them . . . 'it's mine!' When they begin to accumulate excess money, it's mine! Nobody can have it, it's mine!

'Watch out! Be on your guard against all kinds of greed; a man's life does not consist in the abundance of his possessions.' (Luke 12:15)

'He boasts of the cravings of his heart; he blesses the greedy and reviles the Lord. In his pride the wicked does not seek him; in all his thoughts there is no room for God.' (Psalm 10:3-4)

'The treacherous will be caught by their own greed.' (Proverbs 11:6)

'Put to death, therefore, whatever belongs to your earthly nature: sexual immorality, impurity, lust, evil desires and greed, which is idolatry.' (Colossians 3:5)

DISHONESTY . . . 'When you lie, you die . . . to what is honest and honorable!'

Do you remember the name Bernie Madoff? In March, 2009, he pleaded guilty to 11 federal felonies and admitted to turning his wealth management business into a massive Ponzi scheme that defrauded thousands of investors, including many of his friends and associates, of billions of dollars. On June 29, 2009, he was sentenced to 150 years in prison, the maximum sentence allowed.

Perverse? Absolutely! A lying, deadly snare? Undeniably!

'Better a poor man whose walk is blameless than a rich

man whose ways are perverse.' (Proverbs 28:6)

'A fortune made by a lying tongue is a fleeting vapor and a deadly snare.' (Proverbs 21:5)

'The heart is deceitful above all things and beyond cure. Who can understand it?' (Jeremiah 17:9)

'Keep your tongue from evil and your lips from speaking lies.' (Psalm 34:13)

WEALTH . . . 'Wealth or health which will it be?'

Do you remember the story of John D. Rockefeller? At age 54 he was extremely wealthy, but extremely unhealthy! When he began to give away much of his fortune, he began to become healthier. He lived into his 90s . . . obviously he made the right choice.

'Command those who are rich in this present world not to be arrogant nor to put their hope in wealth, which is so uncertain, but to put their hope in God.' (I Timothy 6:17)

'Wealth is worthless in the day of wrath, but righteousness delivers from death.' (Prov. 11:4)

'What good is it for a man to gain the whole world, yet forfeit his soul?' (Mark 8:36)

'He (the wicked man) will no longer be rich and his wealth will not endure.' (Job 15:29)

CONTENTMENT . . . 'It's so plain . . . it's great gain!'

Howard Hendricks once told of the time that he and his wife were invited to the home of a very rich couple who lived in Boston. He was from a 'blueblood' family with connections for years in that city. But Hendricks was surprised that their home was not extravagantly furnished. They had a lovely meal but it was not served on fine china with silverware and crystal. This wealthy couple lived modestly without ostentatious trappings.

Noticing this Hendricks asked him, "How in the world did you grow up in the midst of such wealth and not be consumed by materialism?"

His answer tells it all: "My parents instructed us that everything in our home was either an idol or a tool. We have chosen for our possessions and finances to be tools." Apparently they were content!

History tells us that in 1347 the Black Plague was raging throughout Europe and thousands of people were dying because of it. There were many who considered this to be the judgment of God upon them and their materialistic lifestyles.

So, hoping to appease God's wrath, many citizens of Lubeck, Germany, offered much of their wealth, money, and riches to various churches and monasteries in their city.

The priests and monks inside one of these monasteries fearful of contamination barred their gates and would not allow these citizens to enter. So history records that these persistent crowds began to throw valuables, coins, gold, silver, and jewels over the walls. But the monks threw it all back.

Money and valuables were thrown back and forth for hours until the monks finally gave up and allowed these riches to remain. Within several hours the piles rose to three and four feet high. The interesting part of the story is this: for many months following the incident (some say for years) all this money, jewelry, and valuables remained untouched!

Some say it was because these monks and priests were content to live as they had lived for years; others said that it might have been because of the fear of contamination. But we know that 'godliness with contentment is great gain' . . . greater than possessing items of wealth.

Sometime ago I read these three simple principles that concern contentment:

1.   Seek it! Make contentment your daily choice! Seek to be in the place where 'more' doesn't mean

'happier.' To really be content . . . simplify.

2.   Say it!   Cultivate the ability to say, 'I have enough.'   Push back from the table and say, 'I've had enough.'   Should you receive extra finances that were not expected rather than consider what you now can purchase, why not say, 'I have enough, Lord, how can I use this for You?'

3.   Settle it! David writes, 'If riches increase, do not set your heart upon them.' (Psalm 62:10 NAS) Don't let your excess finances dictate your lifestyle. Choose a realistic level of living and don't compromise. Don't fall for the ads that guarantee you the 'good life' if you buy their product. You already have the really 'good life' when you have contentment. Contentment allows you to live with eternal values in view!

'Keep your lives free from the love of money and be content with what you have.' (Heb. 13:5)

'But godliness with contentment is great gain.' (I Timothy 6:6)

'But if we have food and clothing, we will be content with that. People who want to get rich fall into temptation and a trap and into many foolish and harmful desires.' (I Timothy 6:9)

'Earth has nothing that I desire besides you.' (Psalm 73:25)

GIVING . . . 'Giving is real living!'

Most likely you have eaten some of that 'finger lickin' good' fried chicken from KFC (Kentucky Fried Chicken) where you see the picture of its founder Col. Harlan J. Sanders. KFC's success is due to the Colonel's tenacity and persistence when presenting the right product at the right time.

There is part of his story that you may not know. When he started to sell his 'recipe' for Kentucky Fried Chicken he had little to no money. He was bankrupt and had to sleep in his car when traveling about attempting to make sales to individual restaurants.

But before he began his sales tour he made a vow that he would give 50% of his income to the work of the Lord. Eventually his local church where he was a member, plus many Bible colleges received sizable donations and endowments as well as many individuals having their tuition paid by this successful entrepreneur.

Sanders did indeed give 50% of his profits to God! He became very wealthy, but he never allowed his wealth 'to possess him'; instead he controlled it.

'Each man should give what he has decided in his heart to give, not reluctantly or under compulsion, for God loves a cheerful giver.' (II Corinthians 9:7)

'If anyone has material possessions and sees his brother in need but has no pity on him, how can the love of God be in him?' (I John 3:17)

'If I give all I possess to the poor . . . but have not love, I gain nothing.' (I Corinthians 13:3)

'Give and it will be given to you. A good measure, pressed down, shaken together and running over, will be poured into your lap.'(Luke 6:38)

SAVING AND INVESTING . . . 'Plan your work; work your plan'

'A good man leaves an inheritance for his children's children.' (Proverbs 14:22)

'The plans of the diligent lead to profit, as surely as haste leads to poverty.' (Proverbs 21:5)

'The wise man saves for the future, but the foolish man spends whatever he gets.' (Proverbs 21:20 LB)

'If anyone does not provide for his immediate family, he has denied the faith and is worse than an unbeliever.' (I Timothy 5:8)

WORK . . . 'A good four-letter word'

George spent his early years shuffled between foster homes till one day Maria Watkins, a childless washerwoman, found him asleep in her barn. She didn't just take him in . . . she took him to church and introduced him to Jesus. She also introduced him to what would make him a great man . . . perseverance and a persistent work ethic.

When he eventually left her home, he took with him the Bible she'd given him. Maria left her mark on his life— and George Washington Carver left his mark on the world. This father of modern agriculture was a friend to three presidents of the United States as well as Henry Ford and Gandhi. Carver is credited with over 300 inventions . . . many of them using the lowly peanut. God and Carver developed a partnership that changed the world!

Charles Colson shared this very interesting story while speaking in Jackson, Mississippi:

In 1985 I was on the Bill Buckley television program, talking about restitution and criminal justice. A few days later I received a telephone call from Jack Eckerd, a businessman from Florida, the founder of the Eckerd Drugstore chain, the second largest pharmacy chain in America. (He later sold the chain with approximately 1500+ stores and many of them eventually became CVS stores.)

Eckerd said that he had seen me on television and he asked me to fly to Florida. He agreed that Florida had a criminal justice crisis, would I come down and do something about it? So I did.

We traveled around the state of Florida advocating criminal justice reforms. Everywhere we would go Jack Eckerd would introduce me to the crowds and say, "This is Chuck Colson, I met him on Bill Buckley's television program. He's born again; I'm not. I wish I were." Then he would sit down.

About a year went by and I kept pestering Jack about faith in Jesus. Eventually one day he read some things including the story of Watergate and the Resurrection out of my book, 'Loving God', and decided that Jesus was, in fact, resurrected from the dead. He called me up to tell me he believed. When he got through telling me what he believed, I said, "You're born again!"

He said, "Marvelous!" The first thing he did was to walk into one of his drugstores, walk down through the book shelves and saw 'Playboy' and 'Penthouse' magazines. He'd seen them there many times, but it had never bothered him before. Now he saw them with new eyes. He'd become a born again Christian.

He went back to his office and called his president, saying, "Take all those 'Playboy' and 'Penthouse' magazines out of my stores." His president said, "You can't mean that. We make over three million dollars a year on them." Jack said, "Take them out of my stores!"

Later Colson called Jack Eckerd and asked him: "Did you do that because of your commitment to Christ?" Jack replied, "Why else would I give away $3 million? The Lord wouldn't let me off the hook." Isn't that marvelous? Jack's new partner in business (God) was helping him clean up the business.

When the news got out about this having happened, people all over the country began to shop at Eckerd's drugstores to show their support and within a few weeks their sales were much more than they had been before. Jack was blessed twice: being 'born again' and owning a 'booming business.'

'Commit your works to the Lord and your plans will succeed.' (Proverbs 16:3)

'So whether you eat or drink or whatever you do, do it all for the glory of God.' (I Cor. 10:31)

WHILE INVESTING . . . INVEST IN YOURSELF

People who think of investing only in the terms of money management miss out on possibly the greatest way that investing can produce vast amounts of gain . . . when you invest in yourself! It may sound selfish, but it isn't. Let me explain.

I have for years been blessed by the reading of a daily devotional entitled 'The Word for You Today.' For nearly fifteen years I have had the practice of reading from a current booklet distributed by local churches across America including the Church of Glad Tidings in Austin, Texas. The following paragraphs come from that devotional booklet for November 19:

The scripture for that day was: 'And it was very good.' (Genesis 1:31)

God knew the specific purpose you were born to fulfill, so He provided all the gifts you'd need, including the environment required to put it all together. Then He looked at you and said, 'Very good.' Can you say that, too? It's important that you do. Why? Because others will treat you according to how you treat yourself.

This is not pride, it's just healthy self-esteem based on God's opinion of you as revealed in His Word. When you have it, it affects every area of your life. Truth be told, it determines how far you will go in life. Stop and ask yourself today, 'How do I really feel about myself?' Before you answer read these ten principles.

1. Never think or speak negatively about yourself; that puts you in disagreement with God.

2. Meditate on your God-given strengths and learn to encourage yourself, for many times nobody else will.

3. Don't compare yourself to anybody else. You

are unique, one of a kind, an original; so, don't settle for being a copy.**

4.   Focus on your potential, not your limitations. Remember that God lives in you!

5.   Find what you like to do, do well, and strive to do it with excellence.

6.   Have the courage to be different. Be a God-pleaser not a people-pleaser.

7.   Learn to handle criticism. Let it develop you instead of discourage you.

8.   Determine your own worth instead of letting others do it for you. They may shortchange you!

9.   Keep your shortcomings in perspective . . . you're still a work in progress.

10.   Focus daily on your greatest source of confidence . . . the God Who lives in you!

** Do you realize how really unique and special you are? DNA molecules can unite in an infinite number of ways. The number is 10 to the 2,400,000,000th power. That number is the likelihood that you'll never find somebody exactly like you. If you were to write out that number with each zero being one inch wide, you'd need a roll of paper 37,000 miles long. To put this in perspective, all the particles in the universe are probably less than 10 with 76 zeros behind it—far less than the possibilities of your DNA! Your uniqueness is a scientific fact. When God made you He broke the mold. There's never been and never will be anybody exactly like you!

Investing in your self is wise investing!

John Maxwell in his book entitled: 'Leadership Promises for Your Week' writes the following truths based on the words of Isaiah 48:17 (NKJV)—"I am the Lord your God, who teaches you to profit, who leads you by the way you should go."

In case you're wondering whether or not God wants you to succeed, the answer is a resounding 'Yes!' But you will only succeed if you know and do the right things.

Only as the leader grows, will the company or ministry grow. It's amazing how much time, money, and energy we spend on things that can't produce growth. Logos, websites, brochures, and slogans are all important, but they'll never make up for incompetent leadership. So what should you do?

Once you know that you are walking in God's will and your private life is in order, the keys to success are priorities and concentration.

A well known pastor and business leader offers the following guidelines:

Focus 70 percent of your energy on developing your strengths. Effective leaders who reach their potential spend more time on what they do well than on what they do badly.

Focus 25 percent on new things. If you want to get better you have to keep changing and improving. That means stepping out into new areas. If you dedicate time to new things related to your strong areas, you'll grow as a leader.

Focus 5 percent on areas of weakness. Nobody can entirely avoid working in their areas of weakness. (Note: We are not talking here about sin or character weaknesses that must be dealt with.) The key is to delegate to gifted people the things that you're not particularly good at. That way you're free to concentrate in the areas of your God-given strengths.

When I was a teenager in high school in San Antonio, I did not have the advantage of reading these words or of having the advice shared in the many articles and books that John Maxwell has written and published. But I do remember a specific day when the Lord revealed these truths to me.

I can even now see myself sitting in a classroom as a

student in the ninth grade in Harlandale High School and thinking these thoughts: Focus on your strengths more than you focus on your weaknesses! Accentuate your positives and minimize your negatives. Don't neglect to develop your personality. Be friendly. Be out-going toward others. Invest in relationships.

I remember looking over at two of my classmates who were very bright students, but they had no personality. One of them became the class valedictorian when we were seniors, but she was a 'blah' person who had few friends. The Lord impressed upon me that day that I could study really hard and possibly be the valedictorian or salutatorian, but that it was more important for me to build a network of friends.

Don't misunderstand me . . . I was a very good student . . . I was a member of the National Honor Society. I had scholarship offers. But I also had developed my ability to create relationships with students and faculty members. I was a senior class officer; I was president of the band (musical marching band). I was the editor of the school newspaper. I was selected by the faculty as one of three graduating seniors to receive special recognition and honor. That would not have happened if I had chosen to simply focus on my studies only.

There must be a balance in preparation for the future: invest your mind in studies that will enhance your gifts and abilities; invest your emotions in the enjoyment of music, arts, and dramas that will feed your soul; invest your 'gifts' in whatever makes you feel fulfilled, whether it is in the arts, or the sciences, or the field of physics, or in medicine, or the military, or whatever. The list could go on and on. But don't forget to invest in your spiritual interests through prayer, meditation on the Scriptures, and getting to know God.

As you invest in yourself make sure you have the right people who you will allow to speak into your life. You might want to reread the first Psalm where you are warned about obtaining wrong counsel from the wrong people.

The first three verses of that Psalm say: 'Oh, the joys of those who do not follow the advice of the wicked, or stand around with sinners, or join in with mockers. But they delight in the law of the Lord, meditating on it day and night. They are like trees planted along the riverbank, bearing fruit each season. Their leaves never wither, and they prosper in all they do.' (Psalm 1:1-3 NLT)

That word 'prosper' means stability, nourishment, productivity, strength, durability, and success.

It is so important that you qualify anyone who speaks into your life! Here are seven things to look for: Is this person one who has integrity? Is this person a one who has faith in God? Is this person recognized as an 'influencer'? Does this person share your vision? Is he or she loyal? What about creativity? What about their gifts; are they complimentary with yours?

Be sure to know that you have God's input all along the way. 'Whether you turn to the right or to the left, your ears will hear a voice behind you, saying, 'This is the way; walk in it.' (Isa 30:21)

Your aims, goals, and aspiration must harmonize with God's will for your life; otherwise, all the counselors, coaches, or mentors you may have will not be helpful to you.

Even with all of this working toward your success, is it possible that you may still have what some people call failure? Yes, it's possible, but it may not be a failure. Let me explain.

Realize that your 'failure' may actually be a 'teaching tool' for future success! The greater the 'set back' . . . the greater the opportunity to learn from it! Mistakes and errors can be stepping stones to victory!

Thomas Edison said, "I'm not discouraged, because every wrong attempt discarded is another step forward." At 21 years of age he set up his laboratory in Menlo Park, New Jersey, and became a full-time inventor. At any given time he and his team of fellow inventors were working on as many as 40 different projects.

They applied for more than 400 patents a year! That is outstanding considering that not every project was a success. The fact is that they struggled with many of their projects. But despite failure after failure, they persevered even though there were some ten thousand experiments before finally inventing the incandescent light bulb in 1879.

Edison simply said, "I haven't failed. I've just found ten thousand ways that don't work."

So stop labeling your own failures as negative. There are very few real failures in life—only options! Some options work; some options don't work. Just remember that God is your partner and together you will win if you don't quit.

If you stay focused, you won't quit! Stay focused on the vision that you have been given by God. When you remain focused you will not spread yourself too thin and become mediocre at everything and excellent at nothing. Failure can occur when you continue to say 'yes' to too many projects when you should be saying 'no.'

When your plate is full, be strong enough in your will power to not accept anything that will weaken your resolve. 'No' doesn't mean never, it just means 'not now.' 'No' sets you free from the expectations of others and the need for their approval. Conserve your energy for when it is truly needed to complete your vision.

Yes, I know that Thomas Edison is credited with working on a great number of projects each year, but remember he was wise enough to have a large team of inventors who were working on these various projects. He wasn't working on a multiplicity of assignments alone.

If you allow yourself to not be focused, you may lose the battle. You always lose when you are fighting the wrong battle, or fighting at the wrong time, or fighting when you shouldn't be fighting at all!

Keep your eye on the goal . . . on the prize that God has set before you. If the enemy can't defeat you, he'll distract you with side issues; or he'll disqualify you by getting you to make bad decisions. Either way, he wins and you lose!

Let's take a moment to look at Joseph of Genesis who had to go through the pit and the prison before he arrived in the palace.

Joseph evidently developed himself during his 'down times.' In prison it appeared that his vision was over, but not so. He didn't allow himself to complain and grumble but rather he made himself useful where he was. He was knocked down but he wasn't knocked out.

Interestingly he learned an important lesson while in Egypt . . . when your dream is realized it may be different than you ever imagined. In his dream he saw himself as the 'hero' and his family all bowing down before him. Little did he know that God would not only make that happen, but He would also put Joseph in a position that an entire nation would bow to him.

Because Antonio's voice was high and squeaky, he did not make the tryouts for the Cremora Boys Choir. And he was disappointed. When he took violin lessons, the neighbors persuaded his parents to make him stop. Once again he was disappointed . . . because he loved music.

When Antonio was older he picked up the hobby of whittling and discovered that he had a talent for it. Then he signed on to an apprenticeship with a violinmaker and found that his talent could be used effectively in making violins.

He worked patiently and faithfully at his vocation and became quite good at it. By the time that he died, he left over 1500 violins, each bearing a label that read, 'Antonio Stradivarius.' As you probably know, they are the most sought-after violins in the world. Many have sold for more than an hundred thousand dollars each.

Antonio could not sing or play a violin well, but he did

develop his talent of working with wood and his violins are still making beautiful music today.

Maybe this is a good time to pray this prayer: 'Lord, I realize that you have a dream, a vision for me to accomplish. I know that we are partners and that we can proceed together and succeed together, if I focus on the dream and not become side-tracked. Please help me to remain steadfast even when there are times that I don't understand the path You have chosen for me. I want to trust Your wisdom and Your choices for me even when things look dismal. Give me patience to wait until you open the next door. I realize that true promotion comes from You. Help me not to give up and quit. Help me to persevere until we have the victory. Amen!'

Before we wrap up this chapter there is one more thing that I think is important for us to consider. Give yourself regular check-ups!

Physical check-ups are necessary to maintaining a healthy body. I visit my physician, who happens to be Dr. Thomas Zavaleta, and who has been a personal friend for over thirty-five years. Naomi and I have an appointment with him every six months just for the purpose of a wellness checkup. It usually involves lab work that tests our blood. Yesterday I received the report from his office that our lab tests from last week show that we are in good health. He recommends a low fat, low carbohydrate diet but otherwise we are fine. Thank you, Lord, for good health!

But spiritual check-ups are necessary, too! "Don't drift along taking everything for granted. Give yourselves regular checkups . . . test it out. If you fail the test, do something about it." (II Corinthians 13:5 TM) For good spiritual health you need to regularly check such vital areas as prayer, Bible reading, fellowship, character development, stewardship, and ministry to others. Jeremiah wrote: "Let's take a good look at the way we're living and reorder our lives under God." (Lam. 3:40 TM)

MONEY AND MOTIVATION

We have been focusing primarily on money, finances, savings, and investments . . . but these are not the only important issues in life. We also need to consider our motivations and motives in acquiring riches and wealth.

Making investments must be for a greater cause than simply making money. Making a profit is certainly preferable to losing principal, that's for sure; but 'why do we do the things we do and who do we do them for?' Motives matter!

I believe it is important to invest our finances to achieve a gain for worthy purposes! The question is: What are your purposes in obtaining wealth? Believe me that question is very vital to your long term success! Keep reading . . . you'll be glad you did!

When I think about a man who understands the purpose of making money and investing his life in making financial gains, I think about Truett Cathy, the founder of the highly successful chain of Chick-fil-A restaurants across our nation. Over the years he has become known for growing a very profitable business enterprise and for his faith in Jesus Christ.

He is known for taking a stand that his restaurants would not remain open on Sundays even though it would cost him a loss of millions of dollars in revenue over the years of closure. He is also known for being a faithful Sunday school teacher and for consistently helping many foster children.

In 1982 Chick-fil-A faced a crisis as pressure from other fast food chains caused their revenues to decline. Cathy and his company executives decided to retreat to a resort located on Georgia's Lake Lanier to probe the causes for their problem and seek answers. They decided to focus on this question: 'Why are we in business?' Cathy said they developed this corporate statement: 'To glorify God by being a faithful steward of all that is entrusted to us and to have a positive influence on all who come in contact with Chick-fil-A.' Statistics prove that within the next six months their sales had increased 40%.

Could it be that declaring their partnership with God was vital to their rapid growth and productivity? They think so; and so do I! I think Chick-fil-A is now the largest privately owned restaurant chain in these United States of America.

Yes, there is a segment of our sick society that has viciously targeted Chick-fil-A for Truett Cathy's stand on abortion. There are some universities that have banned the opening of a Chick-fil-A restaurant on their campuses. There are some city councils in Democrat-controlled cities that have done the same. But again and again hundreds of thousands of people who believe in Pro-life issues have participated in highly successful 'buycotts' at Chick-fil-A restaurants to show their support for Cathy. I have been one of them . . . maybe you have, too.

'To glorify God by being a faithful steward' declares who the boss is. God owns it all and we are simply managers of His wealth, His businesses, and His finances. We are stewards!

As I have contemplated this topic, I have clarified in my thinking in several arenas for investments. They are as follows: 1. Finances; 2. Faith; 3. Feelings; 4. Fitness; 5. Faculties; and 6. Family and Friends.

I have not listed them in the order of their importance, because I think all of them are very important. If you fail to invest in any one of these areas, I believe you will suffer loss that could eventually affect your achievements in the other areas.

We must invest our best in all of these in order to truly be productive and fruitful in life.

1.   Finances. We must be good managers of the material blessings we have been given.

2.   Faith. We must carefully nurture the spiritual man; investing in our 'faith-man' through believing prayer, worshipful praise, and fruit-producing Bible study.

3.   Feelings. We must provide adequate nourishment for our emotional needs; because our feelings about life often determines what we think, say, and do.

4.   Fitness. The physical body that houses the soul and spirit must have constant investments of proper food, regular exercise, and adequate rest.

5.   Faculties. We must encourage our mental faculties to grow through inspirational reading, determined study, and educational development. Faculties include our talents and gifts as well.

6.   Family and friends. It is vitally necessary that our relational side be nurtured with times of fellowship and fun with members of our family and our network of friends for our sake and theirs, too. Investment in others always pays great dividends for everybody.

Investment of money into these arenas is money well spent. Some have said that it takes money to make money. And that may be true in most financial ventures, but I have noticed that in many other ventures it also takes investments of time and talent and investments of lots of energy and effort.

Let me tell you the experiences of the first man to ever become a billionaire. He was a man filled with ambition, drive, and connections. By the young age of only 23 he had already become a millionaire and by the ripe middle-age of 50 a wealthy billionaire.

But three years later . . . at the age of 53 . . . he became very ill!

His entire body became one big pain. He began to rapidly lose all of the hair on his head. Although he was the wealthiest man in the world, the world's only billionaire, a man who could purchase anything that he desired . . . he now could only digest crackers and drink milk. He had trouble sleeping for any length of time, wouldn't smile, and found no satisfaction in anything that once brought him meaning in life.

He had a large team of personal, highly regarded, skilled physicians who felt so overwhelmed by his physical condition that they cautiously predicted that he would not be alive in twelve months. That year passed very slowly, agonizingly slow.

As he approached death he awakened one morning with the hazy recollection of a dream. Although he could barely recall it, he knew that it had something to do with the idea that he could not take any of his wealth and material gain with him into the future beyond this present world.

This man was consumed with a passion for making money. He was driven by greedy ambition. He was eaten up with a competitive desire to make more and more money. It was literally killing him! His god was gold and he was a slave to his god . . . and his slavery was rapidly leading to his death!

But this dream touched him deeply and he became convinced he had a choice.

He quickly called his accountants, his mangers, and his attorneys to come to his bedside. When they had all arrived, he made this announcement: 'I want to immediately begin to give away my wealth . . . to research projects, to hospitals, and to missionaries and mission projects. And that very day he set in motion the establishment of the John D. Rockefeller Foundation!

The foundation invested liberally in many causes: the discovery of penicillin, cures for malaria, tuberculosis, and diphtheria. There were numerous other medical discoveries that were also developed and greatly benefitted mankind.

But perhaps the most interesting and amazing part of this story about Rockefeller is this. From the very beginning of his actions to invest his vast wealth in worthy, worthwhile projects to assist his fellowman, John's physical body began to heal!

Yes, he started on the road to recovery. Whereas, at age 53 it definitely appeared that Mr. Rockefeller would not see age 54 . . . he lived to be 98 . . . almost 100 years old.

After his close call with death, he would often teach Sunday school in his local church. On one occasion he made this statement: 'I believe it is a religious duty to get all the money you can fairly and honestly . . . and to give away all you can.' In other words, have a purpose for gaining wealth . . . plan to invest your gains in others, in Christian causes, and in philanthropic programs that benefit mankind to the glory of God.

Truett Cathy and John D. Rockefeller never met each other because they lived in different eras, nevertheless they came to the same conclusion. They learned that investing their treasury, time, and talent to a purpose beyond being a multi-millionaire or even being a billionaire was 'where it's at.' Investment in others for the glory of God is the highest and finest calling!

We all know it isn't money that is the root of all evil, but the love of money. There are men and women who may never become a millionaire even once, but they are consumed by the love of money. They want what it can buy . . . things, more things, prestige, position, popularity, and so forth. They equate it with 'the good life.' They allow that passion to drive them relentlessly. They'll work seven days a week and even devote many evenings to their quest for riches. Who suffers from their unhealthy desire for excessive wealth? They do. Their family members do. Their friendships do.

Truett Cathy asked his team: 'Why are we in business?' What is our purpose? What is our motive?

I have known a number of millionaires over the years. I have seen some who could handle their wealth well; they kept their motives right as they sought first the Kingdom of God and His righteousness. But I have also observed some whose motive for making money was more selfish in nature. I watched as they lost their marriages to divorce. I watched as their children suffered emotional upsets. I watched as a second marriage didn't work out. They didn't have long-term relationships with their friends. They lived fast lives in the fast lane wildly driving to go farther, faster . . . and for what? It was so sad. They were talented, gifted people who invested and did well, but their motivation was unhealthy. And soon it was apparent that their personal lives were unhealthy, too.

Possibly the best way to conclude this chapter on 'Money Motivation' is to quote the admonition of Jesus Christ as found in Matthew 6:33—"But seek first his kingdom and his righteousness, and all these things will be given to you as well."

WHO DOES 'CONSUMERISM' CONSUME?

"Who Does 'Consumerism' Consume" is a catchy title, right? But really, think about it, who is being consumed by consumerism? Is the 'consumer' the customer or the retailer?

According to the Webster's dictionary to 'consume' means to use up, to waste, to destroy, to squander, and to devour. Yet in that same dictionary we are told that the 'consumer' is a person who buys goods or services for personal needs and not for resale. Interesting, huh?

Of course, I know, as most likely you do also, that if you are learning English as a second language, this seems very confusing. Why doesn't 'consumer' mean someone who destroys and who devours something or someone?

Am I making my point? In many cases I think that often big corporate retailers could be 'consumers' of customers by luring them into using up and squandering their money on things or services that high powered advertising or sales persons talk them into buying.

These days retailers are not just 'big box' stores like Walmart but also 'online' stores like Amazon.com. Understand that I have nothing against these stores personally, but I mention them only to illustrate my point. These retailers and many, many others like them have a need for the public to spend money at their stores in order to stay in business. Thus, in this highly competitive shopper's market you the customer (or consumer) is constantly being targeted through advertisements with one purpose in mind . . . they want to consume your money.

In the book 'Affluenza' researchers found that the average consumer (customer) is struck with more than 3,000 commercial messages a day, each one screaming for our attention. Kids will see about one million commercials before they turn twenty, and over their lifetime, all ads strung together would add up to two entire years of watching television commercials.

Such advertising and marketing is not an option for businesses that want to keep their doors open. Today, companies are forced to use every angle imaginable to aggressively compete for your money.

Advertising is big business! 'Affluenza' has reported that the typical thirty-second, national television commercial costs nearly $300,000 to produce—that's $10,000 per second. Here's the kicker. Guess how much it costs to produce one episode of an average television show? About $300,000 . . . approximately the same as a thirty-second commercial! So when you compare the two: $83.00 per second to $10,000 per second, it's a 'no brainer' . . . those commercial ads are highly effective! Make no mistake about it you are being targeted with the best and the finest ads that a creative team can produce.

Then, when you add to that super creative, highly imaginative commercial 'hook' that you are witnessing in the comfort of your home, the likelihood that you will see this ad again and again over the next few days or weeks . . . could result in you being 'hooked.' Repetition works!

Recently as I was driving in my car with the visor down to protect my eyes from the sun I looked up to read on the backside of the visor a message both in English and in French. The French word in boldfaced type was avertissement. This word looked so much like advertisement that I looked twice at it, because next to it was the English translation . . . warning. I immediately thought how appropriate.

Beware! Be on your guard! You are being targeted! You have money to spend and they want to consume it. Attention: when you walk into your den and activate your television, you are entering a battle field . . . just 'watch out' as you watch those cute, appealing ads. Warning . . .

avertissement!

I know that in reality this French word means 'to avert', to keep from happening, to prevent trouble, to turn one's attention away. All of these phrases are indeed appropriate. Naomi and I have the habit of pressing the 'mute' button when the commercials appear. Once you have seen them and heard them, why subject yourselves to them again and again.

In addition to tantalizing you with enticing pictures and sales techniques that have been tried and proven to be winners; some will even lure you with the bait of 'No Payments for Six Months' or '0% Financing'. You are being marketed with an extremely dangerous technique—financing.

Sometimes you may see this one: '90-Days-Same-as-Cash.' Believe me, that is deceptive. Just know that somewhere along the way these contracts that say such things will eight out of ten times convert to monthly payments that could cost you as much as 24 percent interest. And the interest can go back to the date that you made the purchase; thus, you are immediately hit with three months' worth of back interest.

Know that there is more information on financing that can be found in greater detail in Dave Ramsey's book entitled 'Complete Guide to Money', particularly in chapter six entitled 'Buyer Beware.'

Wouldn't we all be much safer living by a budget? What about buying with cash rather than credit? You know, of course, that having credit cards can be as dangerous as swimming with sharks.

Do I have credit cards? Yes, but I pay off my purchases every month . . . there is no interest when the entire amount is paid at the end of every 30 days. I have done this for years. Why not use cash or a debit card? Sometimes I do use cash, but I more often use a credit card that provides me with points or air miles each month. Naomi and I have flown many places over the past many years using miles accumulated through the use of certain credit cards. And we did it with no interest paid to the credit card company. Oh, I slipped up once several years ago and failed to pay my monthly bill on time and was caught. But never again! Now as soon as I receive my bill in the mail, I immediately write my check and mail it to the card company. Why take the chance of that bill somehow being misplaced inadvertently.

Here are some guidelines to safe-guarding yourself as a customer:

- Wait overnight to make that purchase. Have a 'cooling down' period to quietly, calmly consider the ramifications of making that purchase; particularly if it is a major purchase.
- What are your motives in buying it? If it is a pride issue, don't succumb to that trick of the enemy. If it's a 'want' instead of a 'need', is it really the wise thing to do? Some 'wants' are okay, but some are not, so take time to discern which it is. Motives matter.
- What will you forego if you make this purchase? For most families there is just so much money available for making purchases beyond the monthly budgeted items. If you buy this item, what will you not be able to purchase? Which is more important: this or that?
- Take counsel with your marriage partner or a family member or friend. Sometimes they will know of an even better deal. In fact, it is a good habit to investigate several different places where you could make that purchase. The best price may be found somewhere else.
- Have you checked with Craig's List or with a local thrift store? Some of the best buys can be found there.

Jesus Saves! Moses Invests!

My daughter, Cindy Bell, is a very smart buyer. She has made phenomenal purchases by simply shopping wisely and waiting patiently for the best deal possible. Some of her stories of smart purchases are amazing.

I recently asked her to comment about her methods and techniques and here are some of her remarks:

"Unless you have to absolutely purchase brand new, I suggest buying used. Purchasing those same type items from thrift shops for five dollars as opposed to twenty-five dollars plus in a retail store is more my style. You may have to dig a little to find a gem, but then that can be part of the fun.

Learn the names of good quality clothing lines and go hunting. Many people purge their closets regularly, so finding last season's fashion on a thrift shop rack is inevitable.

Not everyone has the eye for this kind of shopping, but if it is something you would like to try, find a friend who seems to spot those deals and go for it.

This is a regular way of life for me and has been for over thirty years. In the early 80's as a newly married couple and still pursuing our education, family finances were tight. My husband and I found every discount we could. Salvage yards, garage sales, church tag sales, and even 'dumpster diving' were added to that list of places where we felt like 'we beat the system.' The hundreds of stories are too numerous to mention.

This I know, my family and I have adopted the biblical perspective that it all belongs to God and He knows what we have need of. Sometimes He even gives us items we would like to have but are not considering a necessity.

My personal testimony bares the fact you cannot out give God! Oh, but how He delights in the challenge.

I keep a running list of needs and wants and have always shopped used first. This is a practice that has been passed down to my children as well.

One Saturday I hurried home from the morning's venture to awaken my sleeping teenage daughter. I eagerly asked her, 'What three things this week did you tell me you needed and wanted?' She replied, 'A T83 calculator, a lighted make-up mirror, and whitening strips for my teeth.' I tossed everything on the bed along with at least ten new items of clothing with the tags still on them. Hundreds of dollars' worth of savings! So before you toss those items into the shopping cart at a retail store, think twice.

I remember once being moved to tears to think my need and want for new washcloths was being supplied in such a sweet way. Just the right color of blue and the lady had even tied them up with the nicest little ribbon. What an opportunity for testimony! Sometimes the most interesting of conversations has happened in someone's front yard or driveway over the exchange of just fifty cents!

Not only for yourself but I encourage you to shop for those you know and love. I have sat on many a couch and held onto an item until a family member or friend has either arrived or verified through a phone, *buy it!*

May you have many happy and interesting shopping trips in your neighborhood or in your local thrift shops. It's a wonderful adventure just around the corner!"

RED BUNK BED

By Cindy Bell (Daughter of Vic Schober)

It happens to all of us. It was a Saturday morning, and being a little too anxious, I almost got ahead of God.

At the time we had four of our five children. The twin girls shared a bedroom and the two boys, being just thirteen months apart, were to be room buddies as well. As I collected items for our recently built home, thoughts of what I needed for a sports themed room for my sons danced in my head. Each visualized idea was quickly becoming a reality.

The first purchase was from a church rummage sale. The old metal school lockers would make for great cubby spaces! Just the right size to hold all the action figures, puzzles Lego sets, books and even the clothing for two little boys. The walls were to be painted a brilliant blue. A perfect backdrop for the primary colored comforters patterned with athletic balls, bats and team pennants. Everything was falling into place perfectly! But now to actually purchase beds.

Of course bright red metal bunk beds were the best possible option I could conceive! Nothing else would do. So much so that I was willing to sacrifice funds for other needs to purchase them new. And in our ten years of marriage this type of purchasing could be counted on one hand.

Almost against our family constitution, we were headed to the credit union at 8:30 that morning to withdraw the needed cash to buy this must have item. But, the Lord, the one who created the universe, rules the nations, and knows me by name had a surprise in wait.

As we rounded the corner, no more than a mile from our home, sat big and bold in a family's front yard the very thing I was headed to buy! Amidst garage sale items of household goods and no longer needed furniture were our bunk beds. The price was $200 less then I had been willing to spend and for $50 the red metal bunk beds were ours.

This was a flagship testimony to the faithfulness of God in the area of stewardship. The extra savings would be given either to missions or a church project. A practice consistent to our family constitution and the continued faithfulness of God for our family continued to go beyond what our minds could conceive.

A 'FIXED INCOME' OR A 'GOD-FIXED INCOME'

Everybody knows or has heard about the constraints of a 'fixed income' . . . especially men and women who are senior citizens dependent on their monthly social security check. But not everybody knows about the freedom of a 'God-fixed-income."

To be a person who lives on a 'God-fixed-income' one must enter into a partner-relationship with the One who creates wealth and riches through creative ideas. A dynamic, imaginative idea could be worth millions of dollars. Ask any successful inventor.

In 1972 I was living in Houston, Texas, where it rains often and grass and weeds grow and flourish very well. Having to mow my yard of St. Augustine grass was a weekly chore that I really didn't relish doing in the Houston humidity. It was difficult having to trim weeds and grassy areas that I couldn't reach with my lawn mower. I often had to crawl on my hands and knees with a hedge trimmer along the fence to get the job done. This, of course, made me susceptible to garden snakes and rodents that could hide in this tall grass. If only there was an easier way to do it!

Little did I know that across town a man by the name of George Ballas was struggling with a similar difficulty. One day as he was taking his car through an automatic car wash, he became intrigued by the circular plastic washing brushes that would clean in between cracks and crevices of the car without doing any damage to the surface. He thought long and hard as to how he could use the idea from the car wash to make a weed eater. He finally came up with the idea of attaching the bottom of a pop corn can with radio wire attached to a wheeled edge trimmer. After a few unsuccessful attempts at making this new device work, he finally got it working, and the 'weed-wacker' began its infancy stages of development. Later when a fellow worker, who was an experienced machinist, helped George put together the idea—the Weed Eater was developed.

Its success is now history! It all began with an idea!

Have you ever read the interesting account of how Velcro was developed? It began with a burcock burr, a tiny seed covered with hundreds of 'hooks' that naturally catch onto the microscopic loops that cover hair, fur, and clothing. The burr was an unassuming marvel of nature and a minor headache for man until one day in 1941 when the burr and Swiss engineer George De Mestral and his dog crossed paths on a hunting trip in the Alps.

Inspired by the burr catching in the hair of his hunting dog, George developed the world's first hook and loop fastener for clothing. Now it has all kinds of usages from attaching your writing tablet to the wall to allowing NASA to keep dinner plates for astronauts from floating off in the weightless atmosphere of their spacecraft.

Why did De Mestral call it Velcro? Velcro is a portmanteau of the French words *velours* (velvet) and *crochet* (hook) . . . thus, a fastening system that is now known worldwide.

It all began with an imaginative idea seen in one of God's creative seeds.

I don't know whether the two Georges that I have just mentioned have given God his due credit for the ideas they developed into very successful businesses; but I do know that Anne Beiler and her husband, Jonas, have done so!

Have you ever tasted one of those scrumptiously delicious Auntie Anne's pretzels? If you have, you know what business I am talking about.

I met Anne several years ago here in Austin, Texas. At the time I was serving as the pastor for her brother, Sam Smucker. Anne shared her testimony with us and we were really thrilled to hear what God had done for her and Jonas.

It all started with a single market stand of baked pretzels in the Downingtown, Pennsylvania, Farmer's Market. Anne had experimented with various recipes and finally settled on one that had occurred somewhat by accident. But, of course, the Lord had something to do with that 'accident.'

At any rate they expanded from one stand to eight stands in Pennsylvania that year, after their first bakery opened in Harrisburg. Then the first mall location was begun in the Park City Center in Lancaster, Pennsylvania, in 1969. By 1992 the Auntie Anne's bakery chain had spread to nine other states with 50 locations. By 2004 there were 887 bakeries in 47 states and twelve countries.

From 1998 through 2010 Auntie Anne's and its franchisees partnered to donate more than $4.5 million to local children's hospitals across the country through the Children's Miracle Network. Auntie's has also supported the pediatric cancer charity Alex's Lemonade Stand Foundation. When Anne sold her business in 2011, there were over 1500 stores in the world.

Anne gives all the glory to God for His idea and His partnership in making her business venture the great success that it is. A few years ago she and Jonas moved to Texas; they now live about an hour's drive from Austin in the Central Texas countryside.

Jonas and Anne Beiler live on a 'God-fixed income'! It pays to partner with God and allow Him to show you His creative, imaginative ideas.

I don't have the space to tell all the stories I know about great men and women who succeeded in business and gave the credit to the Lord for His partnership. But I want to write one more story and then mention several others that you may wish to further pursue on your own.

Do you know the name R. G. LaTourneau? He was a prolific inventor credited with over 300 inventions in the field of large earth moving machinery. He was an excellent Christian businessman and entrepreneur, who lived in east Texas near Tyler.

During my wife's second year as a student at Southwestern Assemblies of God University in Waxahachie, Texas, LaTourneau was one of the chapel speakers that she yet remembers. She told me recently that physically he was a large man and certainly spiritually he was also. He humbly told of his inventions of big earth moving equipment and how on one occasion during his sleep he dreamed of developing one piece of machinery . . . he even dreamed about all the specifications for it. When he awakened, he immediately sketched out what he saw in his dream and later it became a reality as he partnered with the Giver of dreams and ideas.

One of the greatest things that I can say about this great man of God is that the record shows that he lived on 10% of his income and gave away 90% of his wealth to propagate the Gospel throughout the world. He is a prime example of one who knew personally how to live on a 'God-fixed income.'

I want to list several other businessmen who took God as their business partner and gained much from doing so. They learned personally about a 'God-fixed income':

- Bud Paxson . . . Home Shopping Network
- Norm Miller . . . Interstate Batteries
- Sir John Templeton . . . Mutual Fund Pioneer
- Tom Monaghan . . . Domino's Pizza

Oh, I just must tell a bit more about two other Christian businessmen with whom I have had some personal contact:
- David Green, founder of the hugely successful Hobby Lobby chain of stores all across America. I personally know a number of evangelical churches and Christian

organizations that have been given multiplied millions of dollars by David Green to further their ministries for the Kingdom of God. His story is really worth reading!

- Bo Pilgrim, Pilgrim's Pride chicken business. I once met Bo at a special breakfast sponsored by the Texas Republican Party with about thirty-five participants: all the statewide elected officials and many of the top donors who made their elections possible. I was there to open the breakfast with prayer and then enjoy the food and the time of fellowship following the meal. My memory tells me that there were two men with whom I had a conversation that was special and memorable: Senator John Cornyn, who was at that time the Texas Attorney General, and Bo Pilgrim, one of the honored contributors. Both men have made their names known in their fields of service.

I realize that I have given examples of people who have developed their God-given ideas and dreams into large, very successful businesses; but there are untold millions of people who are now living on their God-fixed incomes who have done so in smaller ways. These people whose God-given talents have been exercised in careers for which they were meant to develop. Teachers, engineers, physicians, builders, sales persons, musicians, artists, architects , managers, athletes, and many others have discovered in themselves the talents and abilities to accomplish productive things in life. God generously gave them innate 'giftings' to develop and use them to better themselves. With coaching and education and determination they have become prosperous individuals. If you are one of them, never forget to give God the glory!

When I read in Genesis the story of Adam and Eve and their sons, Cain and Abel, I see the heart of a God who loved them and sought eagerly to partner with them in their lives. He wanted to fellowship with them and enjoy their company. He placed them in a paradise called the Garden of Eden where he generously supplied all kinds of fruit-producing plants and trees for their eating pleasure.

They were given the joy and responsibility of taking care of this garden that showed them the creative genius of their Creator: sowing and reaping, planting and harvesting. They learned that seeds when planted would produce plants that eventually would produce more seeds for more plants. All these were made available to them from the hand of their generous God!

Oh, the genius of it all! God provided the seeds, the ground, and the growing process . . . all they had to do was cooperate with Him and see it all develop more and more. The Bible says that 'Cain worked the soil,' so he learned from Adam what to do, too. It was a gift from the Creator to be passed from one generation to another . . . blessing upon blessing!

Centuries later the Apostle Paul would share with the people of Corinth in his second epistle to them this bit of wisdom: "Remember this: Whoever sows sparingly will also reap sparingly, and whoever sows generously will also reap generously." It is the Law of the Harvest . . . plant abundantly, reap abundantly! Be generous!

The word 'generous' comes from the same base word as the word 'generate'. *Generous* and *generosity* mean the quality of being gracious, magnanimous; willing to give or share unselfishly; rich in yield and fertile. *To generate* is to produce, to beget; the act or process of bringing into being; production.

The Lord wants us to join with Him in partnership to *generously generate* good things in our lives both spiritually and materially. God is very generous; are you?

If you are to be blessed by God, you must be willing to

be a blessing to others. I believe that it is very clear in the Scriptures that we must be generous in our giving, our planting of 'seeds' for others to be blessed, even as we have been blessed.

The Lord Jesus said, "Give, and it will be given to you. A good measure, pressed down, shaken together and running over, will be poured into your lap. For with the measure you use, it will be measured to you." (Luke 6:38 NIV)

I was recently hosting friends for a viewing of a special documentary film at the IMAX theater located in the Bullock Texas State History Museum in downtown Austin when I noticed this quote attributed to Barbara Jordon: 'I get from the soil and spirit of Texas the feeling that there are no limits.' Since I am a Texan, I can appreciate her feelings . . . however I prefer to enhance her statement by saying: 'I get from the soil and the Holy Spirit the feeling that there are no limits with God.'

How about this:

- Natural 'low level', fixed income thinking . . . How many seeds are in an apple?
- Supernatural 'high level' God-fixed income thinking . . . How many apples are in a seed?

I like the idea of living with a 'God-fixed', no limits income . . . how about you?

WHAT DO YOU HAVE TO INVEST?

You can't invest what you don't have . . . so, what do you have to invest? And while we are asking ourselves that question, let's ask a few other questions, too.

So, it simply comes down to what, who, when, where, why, and how.

That's the "Five W's and the H of Journalism". When I took a journalism class in high school, I learned that every lead paragraph in a news story must include as many of the following items as possible: who, when, where, why, what, and how. So, let's cover our 'investment story' by giving attention to the statements listed below.

- First, take an inventory of what you possess that can be invested;
- Second, take God as your partner in this investment;
- Third, make sure it's the right season to make this investment;
- Fourth, take the time to search for the right place to make your investment;
- Fifth, determine your motive for making this investment;
- Sixth, how do you want to make that investment?

Let's look together at the story in the life of Jesus where food was needed to feed thousands of hungry people. The only food found was the lunch of a young boy who miraculously had not already eaten it. It was just five small loaves of bread and two small fish . . . that was it! Andrew, one of the disciples, had discovered it, but 'what is that among so many'?

But the young boy was ready to invest it! So, let's

consider our previous statements.

- First, he doesn't have much but he is willing to invest it . . . 5 loaves and 2 fish.
- Second, he is obviously willing to put it in the hands of Jesus the Son of God.
- Third, the season is definitely right . . . everybody is famished. Food! Feed us food now!
- Fourth, there is no better place to invest than where the Lord desires that you do so.
- Fifth, apparently the boy's motive was to please the disciples and Jesus, not himself.
- Sixth, he wants to give it all to feed the hungry. It's a 100% commitment!

Let's look together at the story in the life of Elisha and the widow of a deceased minister who wants to save her two sons from the consequences of a huge debt that is yet unpaid.

- First, she only has a pitcher of oil and nothing else of any value.
- Second, she agrees to follow the directions of the prophet to find as many empty jars as possible and then to begin filling them with the oil that is poured from the pitcher.
- Third, there is no season riper than one in which there is a crisis. She must act quickly!
- Fourth, the place for the investment just happens to be in her community where she lives. At least she knows her neighbors who will temporarily loan her some empty jars.
- Fifth, her motive was a pure one . . . to save her sons from drastic consequences.
- Sixth, she is willing to pour out all that she has of value . . . 100% of her expendable oil.

In these two examples of investment from which we can draw understanding as to these six questions, let us recognize and discern that these extraordinary results are divine miracle. It would be highly unusual that your investment would have these kinds of miraculous outcome or growth; however, with God all things are possible! Nothing is impossible!

The only thing that Moses had in his hand was a rod used in tending sheep. When the question was asked of him: 'What do you have in your hand?' he submitted his rod to the Lord. Then, the Lord used that rod in outstanding and miraculous ways to free the Israelites that were in bondage in Egypt. The story of their deliverance is packed with one miracle after another!

But are you getting the idea? The questions are simple ones:

- What do you have that can be invested for greater gain? What is in your hand or in your house or in your savings account?
- Are you willing to follow the plan that God is suggesting to you?
- Are you aware that there is a right season for investing, planting, sowing? Timing is important.
- Are you familiar with the place where this investment is to be made? Get all the knowledge you can. Don't go into this project ignorantly or uninformed.
- Your motive needs to be much better than greed . . . 'I just want more and more.'
- Are you willing to totally invest your treasure, time, and talent in this project for His glory if that is required for success? A full commitment is much better than a half-hearted one!

Let's say that you are considering purchasing a small

business.

- First, how much can you afford to invest from your savings? If it takes more than you originally thought it would cost, do you have the excess funds available? Something you could sell? How much can you borrow without endangering your lifestyle?
- Second, are you sincerely seeking the will of the Lord? Is He definitely a partner with you? If God is not with you . . . forget it.
- Third, should you be investing now or should you be doing so at a later time or season?
- Fourth, are you sure you have all the knowledge you need to make the right decisions?
- Fifth, why do want to enter into this investment? Is it for the right motives?
- Sixth, you need to be able to give this venture your best. Being half-hearted rather than giving it your all will almost surely doom your project from the beginning. Give it 100%, nothing less!

In the beginning many investments look really good, but later on seem not as bright as they once seemed. Be prepared to take a 'few hits'! Are your 'pockets deep enough' to make this investment? It may take longer to reach a point of gain or profit than you think? Consider the 'long haul' . . . it's a 'distance race' not just a brief 'sprint.' Often these kinds of investments take years to develop. Some say that must be expected.

If it is an investment in real estate, in most cases it will take three to five years, sometimes ten to twelve years before a good profit can be taken.

In the past three to five years I have purchased three single family houses. I bought them while the market was stressed and appraisals had been lowered each year for three years. Today after waiting for five years for one house, four years for a second house, and three years for the third house, all three have gained in value. One has almost doubled; another has gained about fifty percent; and the third house has gained about thirty-five percent if sold now. It is really a simple formula: buy low and sell high. Each house is leased out presently to good families.

These questions and statements are rather general in nature . . . but be specific in your search for the right answers. Your future success may depend on it! Be thorough! Be diligent! Be steadfast! Be wise . . . seek the counsel of others who have had experience! Seek the wisdom of the Lord through His Spirit's guidance!

Understand that when I speak of an 'investment' it can be one on two levels: spiritual and natural. It can be one that involves specifically the work of the Kingdom of God and it can be one that involves finances and money in the business world. But please know that even when it is an investment for financial gain, it is always best to involve the Lord's wisdom. Never forget that everything belongs to Him . . . you are simply the manager (steward) of His wealth. In the end we will all give an account to Him as to how we managed what He placed in our hands for use. It is an awesome responsibility!

The story is told that General Omar Bradley once made a business trip on a commercial airline wearing a civilian business suit instead of his military uniform. When he was seated, he immediately began working with his file of papers. The man sitting next to him was a much younger Army private who unfortunately did not recognize Bradley.

So after the takeoff the private turned to the general and expressed his opinion that it would be nice if they introduced themselves to each other. He then said that his guess was that the general was a banker.

Not wishing to be rude but needing to continue his work, Bradley said, "No, I'm General Omar Bradley, a five-star general in the U. S. Army. I head up the Joint

Chiefs of Staff at the Pentagon in Washington, D.C."

Without missing a beat, the young private replied, "Well, sir, that's a very important job and I sure hope you don't blow it!"

Your job right now is to seek wisdom and insight concerning your decisions as you invest your money and your life. I sincerely hope you don't blow it!

What a wonderful week Naomi and I had in the beautiful state of Colorado! We loved the mountains, the white-water streams, and the lakes near Durango and Sliverton.

What an impressive family portrait: Cindy and Kermit Bell, my daughter and son-in-law, and their five adult children including marriage partners of four of them with each of these couples showing their less than one-year-old son or daughter. They are all the joy of our lives, especially for my wife, Naomi and me!

These handsome and beautiful people are Jon and Jen Schober, my son and daughter-in-law, and their seven children, my wonderful grandchildren

PROCEEDING TO THE PROCEEDS

If you are 'proceeding', you are advancing on a particular course of action. If your goal is obtaining 'proceeds', you are seeking profits derived from a business venture.

Someone has said that if you aim at nothing, you are sure to hit it!

It is vitally important that you have a goal in mind before beginning to advance. If at all possible (and it is possible), see the end from the beginning. As you start on your adventure, map out as much as possible where you want to go and how you plan to get there.

Some call this a 'business plan.'

Some use what they call a 'decision tree.' It is sketching out the possibilities that are available to you depending on the decisions that you make. If you decide to make a certain choice in establishing your course of action, sketch the consequences that you may endure or enjoy. Then mark out other consequences that might occur if you choose to go a different way. Choices have consequences! Attempt to see them in your mind before you may actually see them occur in reality.

How can that happen? Talk to others who have gone before you on a similar path. Gain from their experiences. Read articles and books in which authors tell their experiences concerning a business that they have founded. Learn vicariously from others' mistakes and from others' successes. Don't reinvent the wheel!

To launch out in a new business without any previous experience in that line of work is extremely risky. There are many pitfalls to confront in establishing any business, so proceed very cautiously and carefully, wisely gain all the information you possibly can before commencing to step out with your 'proceeding.'

The old 'master and apprentice' type of education was exceptionally wise. It was a 'show and tell' approach to learning. Eventually the apprentice would have had enough training and personal experience to go out on his own. The medical profession still uses this type of preparation for physicians when they have young doctors in a 'residency program.' Some call this an 'intern program.' I have heard of some, who in order to gain knowledge and insight into a particular business, would offer to work for nothing (no pay check) simply to learn the business through experience. I would think 90 days would be the maximum.

You may wish to consult a CPA before investing your money in any venture. He or she will have a lot of advice to share that will prove to be very profitable in the long run.

You may wish to consult an attorney for the best approach to establishing your business venture. These days there are so many laws and regulations placed on you by various branches of the government at the state level and at the national level. Know what they are before you unwittingly break them. The law will not excuse you for ignorance. Those who enforce the law will say that you should have known . . . and then they will proceed to fine you.

Breaking the law is breaking the law, whether you do so knowingly or unknowingly. Stupidity and ignorance may seem to be similar, but they are different and you may still have to pay the consequences either way. Oh by the way, 'stupidity' is knowing something to be so and still advancing as if there would be no consequences to pay. 'Ignorance' is simply 'not knowing the truth.'

Here is an example: You are driving in a heavy rain storm and for several days this kind of weather has prevailed. As you continue driving you approach a sawhorse with this sign attached to it: 'Warning! Flood waters ahead!' 'Stupidity' ignores the sign and continues driving full speed ahead. 'Ignorance' is either being careless and not reading the sign or it is being illiterate. No matter which is the case . . . if you continue driving without slowing down or stopping, there is danger ahead. Watch out! Beware!

Everybody who enters into a business arrangement, whether it is establishing a new business, entering a partnership, buying stock in a corporation, or seeking employment . . . don't be ignorant or stupid . . . gains all the information that he can before acting.

Let's say you are thinking of opening a restaurant. Here is a partial list of things to consider:

- The cost of the lease on the building
- The cost of insurance
- The cost of utilities
- The cost of advertisement
- The cost of employees
- The cost of food products
- The cost of maintenance
- How effective are your competitors? Will you 'out-do' them?
- What will happen if the government decides to raise the minimum wage?
- Who will keep accurate records for paying FICA taxes and other taxes?

I don't want to seem pessimistic or negative, but all of these are legitimate concerns that must be considered. And this is just a partial list.

However, in order to progress in any venture, there is always a risk involved . . . maybe several risks that must be taken. Sometimes it is worth taking the risks. Nothing ventured; nothing gained!

During my teenage years my immediate family lived in San Antonio, Texas. My mother's sister and family, my uncle and aunt, Cecil and Flo Beard, and family lived about 100 miles north of us in Austin. For many years Uncle Cecil was an employee of Southern Gas Pipeline and had a good job with an excellent salary. They were a stable family who enjoyed the benefits of a stable company.

One day four of Cecil's fellow employees approached him with the offer to join them as they quit their jobs with Southern Gas Pipeline and started a new company. They explained to him their plans and how they felt they would succeed in their new venture. They wanted him to be in partnership with them. When they talked with him, it really seemed like a great opportunity.

But when Cecil explained it all to Flo, she wasn't as excited as he was. She expressed her fears that their monthly paycheck would no longer be a regular, dependable paycheck. She brought up the fact that he would no longer have a retirement plan. What if this new business didn't succeed? What if they loss all their savings? What if they would have to move to find another job? There were lots of questions . . . legitimate questions.

The bottom line is this: Cecil and Flo decided to punt. They felt safer with his employment with Southern Gas Pipeline.

My aunt many years later shared this story with me and she told me about that sick feeling she felt in the pit of her stomach each time she saw that world famous logo: 'T I' (Texas Instruments). They could have been one of five couples who started Texas Instruments!

They had opportunity knock at their door, but allowed all those nagging questions to overwhelm them . . . and they refused to answer the 'knock.'

Of course, hindsight is always 100% correct. 'If only' is always the wail given when a terrific opportunity comes your way, but you let it slip through your fingers.

Somewhere between weighing out the possibility of fumbling the ball against the possibility of making the big touchdown that wins the game . . . there is that all-important-decision to 'go for it' or 'punt.' Cecil and Flo punted.

In retrospect you might groan out: "Why didn't they go for it?" But the bigger question is: "If you had been in their shoes that day in Austin in the 1950s, what would you have done?"

That's a tough decision to make . . . since you don't know the future. But that is always the case, isn't it? 'Tomorrow' . . . will it be for better or for worse? For richer or for poorer?

My best advice in facing 'tomorrow' is to face it 'knowing God can guide you each step of the way.' Trust Him! Acknowledge Him in all your ways! Don't lean solely on your own wisdom! Search out God's wisdom and the wisdom of a multitude of counselors.

'Going for the touchdown' or 'going for the gold' will always have certain risks. Rarely is an action on your part a 100% sure thing. But having God as your partner greatly minimizes your risks. Should you seem to fail, don't consider it a 'failure'; consider it as another lesson you learned in order to eventually achieve your goal.

Jesus Saves! Moses Invests!

PARTNERING WITH PROVIDENCE

My original intention in writing this chapter was to focus solely on the opportunity that is ours to be in partnership with 'divine providence.' However, when checking more closely as to the definition of 'providence' I discovered something quite interesting.

- Definition #1 is: a looking to, or preparation for, the future; provision
- Definition #2 is: skill or wisdom in management; prudence
- Definition #3 is: the care or benevolent guidance of God.

Suddenly I am given a three-point outline of what this chapter should now consider!

- First, let's consider that we should wisely prepare for the future by making provision for any eventuality.
- Second, let's consider the prudence and wisdom of developing managerial skills.
- Third, let's consider the importance of seeking the care and guidance of our benevolent God.

Provision for the Future!

Have you ever heard of a myrmecologist? No, it is not a person who studies 'murmuring.' Myrmecology is the study of ants. I'm not sure that devoting one's life to studying these insects is what I would want for a grandchild of mine; however, I do know that the Bible says we should consider the way of the ant.

They are amazing creatures and there is much wisdom that we can learn from them.

Let me share just a few facts about them:

- There are over 10,000 different species of ants.
- They are able to lift over twenty times their body weight.
- They have been found to build structures 500 times their own height.
- The brain of one ant has 250,000 cells, whereas the human brain has 10,000 million cells. It has been said that ants probably use more of their cells than we do.
- Ants have two stomachs: one for storage to share later and one for food for itself now.
- An ant has a life expectancy of just 45-60 days.

I recently read an account of a missionary from India who had learned some lessons from the ant. The story goes: "The Lord must have desired to teach me something through the 'ants' because He allowed me to come in contact with so many of them. The encyclopedia says there are more ants than any other insect. It seems to me that most of them must be in India!

Everywhere I look, I see ants. There are ants in the plastic bag of bread even though it is securely tied. There are ants in a jar of jam even though its lid is screwed on. There are ants in a tin box of cookies even though its lid was tightly fastened. Ants, ants, and more ants everywhere all day long.

By evening I am thoroughly annoyed. I have eaten ants in my breakfast, in my lunch, and in my dinner. Hoping to get a good night's sleep, I have moved my cot out into the open, away from the tent and the trees, but as I lay down with a sigh of exhaustion, I am soon jolted from my rest by the fiery bites of more ants."

There are two interesting scriptures concerning ants in the Bible:

- "Go to the ant, you sluggard, consider its ways and be wise! It has no commander, no overseer or ruler, yet it stores its provisions in summer and gathers its food in the harvest." (Proverbs 6:6-8)
- "Ants are creatures of little strength, yet they store up their food in the summer." (Proverbs 30:25)

It is obvious by observing them that they are not procrastinators. They don't wait until the weather turns cold before they begin their preparations. They gather food while it is still warm. They diligently prepare for the future and for their families.

In addition to their industriousness in preparations, they are also great examples of perseverance. They have this amazing ability to survive all kinds of circumstances whether it's dangerous weather conditions or disasters to their anthills because of a lawn mower or having their anthill kicked or washed away by a water hose . . . they immediately begin 'building back'. They are not quitters!

One naturalist has written: 'On their own each ant's behavior is relatively useless, but when swarms of ants come together, the patterns optimize naturally and it allows them to accomplish tasks that should be far beyond their reach. To the outside observer their self-organizing efforts seem to be directed by some larger force or collective intelligence. Theirs is a society that is truly more than the sum of its parts.'

Did you catch that phrase . . . 'larger force?' I believe that force is God himself who created the ant and placed within it the desire to fulfill its purpose. So, we see that partnership is needed to accomplish provision for the future.

One article I read in my research for this chapter stated that there are several lessons we can learn from the ant:

- The ant is determined! Ants are not easily deterred . . . they continue to seek ways to succeed.
- The ant is an opportunist! They will use a stick or a leaf or a straw from an old broom to navigate over terrain that is not passable.
- The ant will communicate effectively! Whenever one ant finds something of value, it sends out a message to all other ants to join with it in gathering crumbs of food.
- The ant is concerned for others! They are notorious for being cooperative one with another; just watch an ant colony at work.
- The ant is definitely not single-minded! Rarely do you see 'lone ranger' ants. They seem to work best in teams.

But with all of this information, please keep in mind that 'provision for the future' is the number one mandate! Think ahead! Provide for your 'tomorrows.' Wisely plan for next month, for next year, even for the next decade . . . and certainly for eternity!

Prudence in Management!

In my book entitled: 'Add ZING to Your Quest for Maximum Success' I talk about the importance of teamwork. Teamwork makes the dream work! I will not repeat that chapter here, but I do recommend the book as a great source for learning teamwork.

Good management skill involves delegation of

authority! I know by personal experience how important it is to complete a big project by involving others who can share in the responsibilities.

Through the years of my pastoral ministry in Houston and then in Austin, I learned that I did not have all the skills necessary to do a first-rate job. I had certain talents for speaking, teaching, and writing. I also had some talents in music: singing and playing the piano. It was forced upon me to be a business manager, but not having formal training in accounting, I was at best just mediocre.

At the Gulfgate Assembly of God Church in Houston, when we launched a building program to construct a new sanctuary and educational wing, I was so relieved that we had a deacon board member who had skills in construction and could serve as our representative with the contractor we had hired to build the new building. Thank God for Charles Mead!

When I became the district youth director for the South Texas District, I needed an administrative assistant who could bring it all together and God provided Marie Bunker. We had several big projects each year, such as five weeks of youth camps, a large annual youth convention at a hotel, and two Ambassador in Mission trips overseas each year. One of the AIM trips involved 275 people going to Monterrey, Mexico, and another one involved 195 'AIMers' spending a week in Tampico, Mexico. Having a skilled administrator in Marie was vitally important to the success of all these ventures. Of course, there were many others who worked with me as the director as we mobilized and motivated these teenagers to witness to thousands of Mexicans each day and then become a giant choir in nightly services where many hundreds of people would come to hear our music and an anointed minister share the Gospel.

Bringing off fruitful youth camps involved a large team of people who worked with me each summer at the Pearl Wheat Campground near Kerrville (now named Hill

Country Camp). Wonderful people like Sonny and Margie Jaynes and Dowie and Twila Johnson . . . and many others. Youth camps involved not only services at night in the open-air tabernacle, but sports and games for the over two hundred campers who were with us each week; and we had to purchase food then prepare, and serve three tasty meals each day for five days each week. It demanded that I have dozens of workers to bring off successful camps. God helped me to have willing workers and counselors to whom I could delegate authority in many areas.

When I left that assignment at the district after four years of service, Naomi and I were led by the Spirit to plant a new church in northwest Houston near Spring, Texas. I am so thankful to Him that our youth camp executive team joined with us to be the team of ministers who planted the Church of the Trinity. What a great twenty months we had together! The congregation grew rapidly from about 35 people to over 200 people in that short length of time.

Again I learned the value of 'team'! Among other programs we instituted we had exciting 'Sunshine Fairs' for children in various neighborhoods that resembled a cross between a Backyard Sunday School/Kids Krusade/Kids Camp all wrapped up in one. We would have a parade through the neighborhood on bicycles and cars with banners and signs inviting kids to join with us for this fun-filled event for Christ. Sometimes we would have over an hundred boys and girls participating. It could not have happened without a group who individually had been delegated to various positions and assignments. We were a team!

After the Church of the Trinity, we Schobers moved to Austin, Texas, to become the senior pastors at the Church of Glad Tidings. Again I learned that it could not be done without an adequate team of talented people. At one time we had twelve ministers on the pastoral staff, each with different portfolios of ministries. Prudence in management was essential to our being an effective and productive leadership team for the congregation.

I remember once challenging the pastoral staff to do as I had done: I had delegated and organized an effective team (meaning them) and now I wanted them to organize a great team of volunteers and be prudent in management of them. They responded positively and at one point we had over four hundred people working together in many different teams to minister to children, teens, college students, couples, men, women, and families. Those were blessed days.

Now Pastor Kermit Bell, who is the senior pastor at GTaustin (Church of Glad Tidings) has not only maintained a vibrant central congregation but also established several growing PAC (parent affiliated churches) congregations in the Greater Austin area. It could not have been done if it were not for prudence in management on the part of Pastor Kermit and his experienced staff of directors, pastors, and deacon board members.

Providential Guidance by God

If I developed a website for this purpose, I might call it 'G.O.D. Global' (God Ordained Directions Global!) We could then access 'providential guidance by God' anywhere in the world and feel secure in knowing that the Spirit was giving us up-to-date information. Who to see! Where to go! What to do! What to say! When to act! Although a website might be a very useful tool, we have something even better: we have the Holy Spirit. He is willing and able to provide guidance, instruction, insight, and much more. And He is always available anywhere and at anytime of the day or night.

Since the major thrust of this book concerns investing, we definitely need providential guidance in the adventure of putting finances into a venture for profit.

Does God care whether we profit or not? Read Isaiah 48:17—"I am the Lord your God who teaches you to profit, who leads you by the way that you should go."

Then, in I Timothy 6:17 Paul exhorts us to wisely use our profit and wealth. "Command those who are rich in this present world not to be arrogant nor to put their hope in wealth, which is so uncertain, but to put their hope in God, who richly provides us with everything for our enjoyment."

He then expands on that thought with this admonition: "Command them to do good, to be rich in good deeds, and to be generous and willing to share. In this way they will lay up treasure for themselves as a firm foundation for the coming age, so that they may take hold of the life that is truly life." (vv. 18, 19)

When seeking the guidance of the Spirit in making decisions of any kind including decisions about financial matters, you may receive guidance in many ways, including:

- The Word of God (Bible scriptures made very real to you)
- The Holy Spirit (the still, small voice in your spirit and soul)
- Sermons and songs (phrases that resonate in your thinking)
- Casual conversations (thoughts and ideas shared through others by the Spirit)
- Words of counsel (people who have spoken into your life)
- Dreams and visions (God-given spiritual directions)
- Bible studies and articles (what others have written; testimonies)
- Unusual ways (a message on a billboard, on a magazine ad, or in a film)

In most cases I suggest that you have two or three 'witnesses' collaborating. Don't move forward on just one of the above. Get confirmation from several sources.

When you are sincerely, eagerly desirous of hearing from the Lord as to what, when, and where, etc. just know He will respond. He loves to communicate with His family!

Today's 'Global Village' and 'Information Superhighway' began many years ago with a young artist named Samuel Morse. The son of a minister, Morse sailed to London at age 19 to study art. He became acutely homesick and wrote: 'I wish that in one instant I could tell you of my safe arrival, but we are 3000 miles apart and must wait four weeks to hear from each other.'

Morse became a respected artist and portrait painter, but his life took a sudden turn in 1832 as he traveled back to America aboard the steamship Sully. As God would have it one night the conversation at his dinner table turned to the sending of electric messages along a length of wire. Morse was seized with the idea . . . an idea that God had obviously planted in his soul.

He arrived home, took a room atop his brother's newspaper building and spent every spare moment diligently working over his 'Tele-Graph.'

After years of trial and error, Morse prepared a dramatic demonstration. He laid two miles of water-proofed wire under New York Harbor; but unfortunately, a ship's anchor caught the wire and destroyed it, and the crowds left, muttering.

But Morse planned an even more dramatic demonstration for the United States Congress. On May 24, 1844, before assembled dignitaries, he sent a message from the U.S. Capitol to the railroad depot in Baltimore. The first telegraph message consisted of four words from Numbers 23:23—"What hath God wrought."

All America and Europe were soon linked by telegraph

wires!

"It is all of God," Morse later said. "He used me as His hand in all this. I am not indifferent to the rewards of earth and the praise of my fellow men, but I am more pleased with the fact that my heavenly Father has allowed me to do something for Him and for His world. Not unto us, but unto God be all the glory. Not what hath man, but what hath God wrought!"*

This is but one of many such stories that exist because of providential guidance by God. He is still in that business! Take Him as your business partner and 'partner with providence.'

*I found this wonderful story recently in a devotional book that I have had in my library for over fifteen years: "From This Verse" by Robert J. Morgan, Thomas Nelson Publishers.

SURGE OR PURGE?

Decisions, decisions . . . do I charge forward, full speed ahead . . . or do I pull back and stop what I am doing? What should I do? Push the pedal to the metal or shut the engine off?

Or is there a third option? Maybe it is to seek advice and counsel from a qualified, mature person who may be able to suggest another alternative. Sometimes there is something that can be done that does not require such drastic action, like surging ahead or purging (quitting) totally the project at hand.

"In the multitude of counselors there is safety," says the wise man in Proverbs 11:14. You might want to seek advice from several people.

The answer may simply be to have patience and wait!

The market could be making a 'correction' and then in a few days it will continue to climb. To act too quickly may be a mistake.

If you have invested in an automobile or real estate with the idea of selling it for profit (which is sometimes called 'flipping it'), but you have not sold it as quickly as you had thought you would, be patient. It only takes one buyer, he may come tomorrow. Don't panic!

Many a person has acted too rashly one day only to regret it a day or two later. 'If only I had waited a little longer' is not a statement you want to be making regretfully next week.

Your counselor may have a suggestion or two for better advertisement. Or he may be able put you in contact with a network of people who can be of assistance.

There can be any number of choices available to you beyond what you now know.

Have you prayed about it? Ask for wisdom from the Lord. I know, some people think that prayer means you have come to your wits' end and it is now an action of the 'last resort'. But prayer should be one of the first things you do, you keep doing, and you don't stop doing whatever your project.

Prayer changes things. Prayer puts God in partnership with you. He can make the difference. His guidance by the Spirit can direct you. It is possible to have a 'Spirit-led nudge' that prompts you to maintain your course of action or go forward with due diligence or stop completely. You can have a 'peace' that is from the Lord when you make the right move . . . and continue to have that peace. 'Sink or swim' choices are scary. But float with God and know His peace. Remember, when He is involved, you are more than a conqueror!

THE KEY TO LIVING A LIFE OF AUSTERITY OR PROSPERITY?

What are we talking about . . . austerity or prosperity? Webster's dictionary says this:

- 'austerity'. . . a tightened economy with shortages of consumer goods
- 'prosperity'. . . an economy of wealth and plenty
- Words like this describe austerity: to be in want, deprivation, difficulty, low estate, forced simplicity.
- Words like this describe prosperity: abundance, plenty, well-fed, more than enough.

The Apostle Paul spoke of knowing and living at times in each of these conditions:

" . . . I have learned in whatsoever state I am to be content. I know both how to be abased and I know how to abound: everywhere and in all things I am instructed both to be full and to be hungry, both to abound and to suffer need. I can do all things through Christ who strengthens me." (Philippians 4:11-13)

But the key to 'living the good life' is contentment while living in either of those circumstances!

Cindy Bell, my daughter, after visiting and ministering to people in Uganda, said that she was really impressed by the obvious joy of the Christian Ugandans. She said that they had only the basic necessities of life: a bed, a table, a chair . . . a few simple changes of clothes . . . a simple meal maybe twice a day; but in their deprivation . . . they had exuberant joy and contentment. They had gladness of soul! They were not disgruntled, unhappy people.

How can that be? Obviously they had learned that they could do all things through the Spirit of Christ. The Phillips translation says: "I am ready for anything through the strength of the one who lives within me."

Are you discontent or content in your spirit? Happiness in life should not be dependent on whether we have less or we have more . . . happiness is a choice . . . it is an attitude that we choose. Making a decision to live positively rather than negatively is up to you!

"This is the day that the Lord has made; I will rejoice and be glad in it!" Never forget: "The joy of the Lord is your strength."

Should there be another recession or depression economically in our nation . . . may we have an expression of contentment upon our countenance because deep within us there is a '(will) well of satisfaction' from which we are drawing living water and we choose to be satisfied!

WILL IT MAKE YOU OR BREAK YOU?

Not every financial investment is successful! There is always the possibility that an investment that looked really good when you 'bought into it' can be a big disappointment. Rather than making a profit, you suffer a loss. That always hurts! Now what?

Now you have the opportunity to learn some great lessons through tough times!

Adrian Rogers, the great Baptist minister in Memphis, Tennessee, once wrote the following:

Here is what you learn in tough times:

1. Enjoyment. "Count it all joy when you fall into trials." (James 1:2) It's when you pass God's test that He fills you with His joy. So pull some of the groans out of your prayers and throw in a few 'Hallelujahs.' Remember, pain is inevitable—misery is optional!

2. Enlargement. The Psalmist wrote, "Thou hast enlarged me when I was in distress." (Psalm 4:1) Most of the things we know best, we learned the hard way. Often our greatest progress comes from our greatest pain, hence God doesn't save us from it, He strengthens us in it.

3. Enlightenment. The Bible says, "Unto the upright there arises light in the darkness." (Psalm 112:4) We don't realize how little we know until we walk through some dark places and God turns on the light.

4. Endurance. James writes: "See how the farmer waits for the land to yield its valuable crop and how patient he is for the autumn and spring

rains. You too be patient and stand firm." (James 5:7-8) You can't shorten the seasons or hurry the harvest, so be patient. And pay attention. While you are waiting, God is working.

Bruce Wilkinson says: 'Tests of faith through trials and hardships invite you to surrender something of great value to God, even when you may have every right not to.'

All sinners can be winners! Yes, all have sinned and fall short of the glory of God. To 'sin' in archery simply means to 'miss the mark.' So, sinner, when you aimed for personal success in your life and you missed the mark by falling short of your goal, you can still become a winner! Turn to God in your loss, He can be a 'present help in time of trouble.'

Ask God to help you. Ask Him to forgive you if you have willfully committed sin. Maybe your failed investment was due to foolishness on your part. Maybe you didn't ask His will in your actions. Maybe you had the wrong motives when you acted. Maybe you have been greedy and selfish. Confess your sins and seek His counsel! You can still be a winner in Christ!

WHAT'S THE 'TAKE AWAY'?

What do I mean when I say the 'take away'? In business it means your 'net profit' . . . your bottom line reward.

Okay, you are a very busy, industrious, addicted-to-work kind of person. Here's something you need to consider before they make plans for your funeral service and they place wreaths of flowers around your grave . . . if you are living only for the rewards offered to the successful in this life here on planet earth, you might not be too happy with the 'take away'. All the hard work and long hours you spent on one project after another may not be worth the investment.

One very wise man once wrote: 'So I turned in despair from hard work. It was not the answer to my search for satisfaction in this life. For though I do my work with wisdom, knowledge, and skill, I must leave everything I gain to people who haven't worked to earn it. This is not only foolish, but highly unfair.' This quote is from Ecclesiastes chapter two and verses 18 through 21 in the New International Version.

Author John Capozzi wrote it this way: 'The executive who works from 7 a.m. to 7 p.m. seven days a week will most likely be considered by many to be a successful businessman. He will also be fondly remembered by his wife's next husband.'

The day when you leave it all behind is closer today than it has ever been. The fact that you have been stressed, strained, and driven to accomplish and to achieve your goals will not matter on the day after your last day here on earth. Adding another 'win' to your resume won't matter anymore. Making another big deposit in your bank account won't matter anymore. Investing in another project to see how much 'take away' can be achieved won't matter anymore. Why? Because you can't take any of it with you!

When John D. Rockefeller died, someone asked, "How much did he leave?" Someone else answered, "All of it!"

A number of years ago Naomi and I thoroughly enjoyed a cruise that took us to several very interesting countries that included Spain, Monaco, Greece, and Italy. While cruising around Italy we spent a day each in the delightful cities of Venice, Rome, and Pompeii.

Pompeii was where Mt. Vesuvius erupted in A.D. 79 with volcanic molten lava and hot ashes spewing forth and killing most of the residents of the city. Several years ago some construction workers discovered another corpse outside the ancient city. This woman like many others was trying to escape but didn't make it.

The workmen found that this woman's hands were clutching a fistful of jewels. The jewels had survived, but she had not. The same is true today. There will be a day when we exit this life and we will leave behind every possession that we have considered valuable and important.

Wise men and women, who know there will be this 'day of exit', plan a 'take away' that includes these three things:

1. Satisfaction . . . that you have fulfilled your God-given assignment while living here on earth. It's not how much you kept, but how much you invested in others.
2. Success . . . that is measured in these terms: you did all you could with what you had to the glory of God! Only what's done for Him will last; all else will pass away!
3. Security . . . that deep settled peace in your soul that all is well between you and your Maker!

Believe me, these are definitely the only 'take away' items that really matter . . . that truly will count in eternity!

'The Deal of the Decade'

In 1976 a new chapter in the twenty-five year old Church of Glad Tidings, Austin, began in January of that year as Naomi and I moved from Houston to become their new pastors. I preached my first sermon to a church full of nearly 200 congregants as they all looked eagerly forward to the future.

Within three years a new sanctuary seating over 450 was constructed next to the older church and educational wing. It was dedicated to the Lord in 1978. By the tenth year of my pastoral ministry in 1986 the church was meeting on Sundays with three morning worship services and the parking lots were overflowing with automobiles, also with parking up and down the streets surrounding the church property. It became quite evident that new facilities and larger parking lots were desperately needed and soon.

After attempting to purchase more property adjacent to our present location and finding that attempt thwarted; and then trying to purchase property across the street and having that attempt also thwarted; we were perplexed. Evidently relocating was the only option that remained, but the big question was where!

The second largest Baptist church in Austin, the Allandale Baptist Church, had relocated several miles away which became the Great Hills Baptist Church. They were now willing to sell their Allandale buildings for $2,700,000. So, the church leaders and I took a tour of the five buildings (about 90,000 square feet in total) and considered purchasing it. These buildings were just about one mile from the present location for Glad Tidings at 2000 Justin Lane.

But what happened in the next few years would become 'the Deal of the Decade.' Glad Tidings did not immediately purchase the Baptist church facilities; but to make this story as short as possible, asbestos was discovered in all of the buildings and that changed everything!

The Baptists, which still owed on the Allandale buildings, let it go back to the bank. Then the bank held the title deed for several months, but soon the bank went into receivership to the Federal Assets Management Corporation. Now we as GT leaders would have to deal with the federal government!

Eventually the property went on the auction block literally on the steps of the Travis County Courthouse in May, 1990. That's where the miracle took place!

We had scrounged up all the money we could . . . a little over four hundred thousand dollars. We would have to pay cash that day, if we won the bid.

As it happened we were one of three groups that would bid on the Allandale buildings. There were two different lawyers representing two different investment groups and they each had a lot more cash reserves than GT had. Oh, God, please help us!

The bidding began quite low. First, one group bid one thousand dollars above the low starting bid; then, the other group bid one thousand dollars above that bid. Our GT attorney had been instructed to make strong bids, so he bid five thousand above the previous bid. This pattern continued for several rounds, when one of the opposing lawyers called for a five-minute recess. He spoke to the other investment attorney saying that they were there just to make money and that they ought to back off and let the 'church people' buy the 'church buildings.'

An agreement was reached and when the bidding resumed, no one 'topped' the last bid that GT had offered. Going once, going twice, going three times . . . Glad Tidings bought the Allandale church facilities for $270,000 . . . about ten cents on the dollar from what had been the original sales price of $2,700,000.

A triumphant shout of victory arose from the thirty or so GT people who had gathered on the steps of the courthouse. It was a great day for all of us from Glad Tidings!

Within less than a year the asbestos was abated from all five buildings at a cost of about $350,000; then, a little over a million dollars was spent in remodeling and refurbishing the five buildings. And the congregation moved into their new location on Northland Drive just before Christmas. What a marvelous Christmas gift that God had given to His people called Glad Tidings!

But that's not the end of the story! There was included in the properties that were in the final bid five lots across the street from the church campus. For years the GT congregation would unofficially use those lots for overflow parking from time to time. But those lots were to be a second miracle blessing in the future!

In 2014 a national major house building corporation approached GTaustin with an offer to purchase those five lots so that they could build five single-family houses on them to sell to five different families. After discussing the offer thoroughly and bringing it to the congregation for their approval, GT and the corporation reached an agreement as to the selling price: $1,634,000. What a generous, generous gift God had given to Glad Tidings! This sum was approximately the amount that GT had originally spent back in 1990 in purchasing the 2700 Northland Drive property, then abating the asbestos, and remodeling the facilities! In essence the entire five buildings and property was a totally free gift! Oh, you should know that those facilities are now valued at between fourteen and fifteen million dollars! It really was the 'deal of the decade'!!

I thank the Lord for two men who untiringly gave of themselves to make this happen: GTaustin's present pastor, Kermit Bell, who at that time was the assistant pastor, and Steve Van Winkle, who was at that time a member of the deacon board and the attorney for GT.

INVEST IN 'MAXIMIZING OTHERS'

My son, Jonathan, really believes in 'maximizing others' . . . so much so that he has a website by that name and the recording on his cell phone's answering service for voice mail indicates the same, too. He is in the business of assisting others to become all that they can be . . . he is a personal coach. He also does business coaching for managers and owners of small businesses.

I had an inspiring lunch with him and two successful businessmen recently and thoroughly enjoyed our almost two hour conversation over tasty Mexican fajitas with all the condiments. While Jon was away from the table to take a phone call for a few minutes, one of the men spoke to me of his personal admiration for Jon and his ability to easily meet people from all walks of life. He commented about his observations of Jon and his genuine desire to help others develop and grow better in their personal and public lives.

Of course, I was very pleased to hear his complimentary remarks about my son.

Jon's wife, Jennifer, is a great match with Jon . . . they both have invested in the lives of many individuals and couples even entire families. I can think of a number of incidences in which the young Schober family hosted one, two, and even five or six people at a time in their home for several weeks. Some were family members but most were friends who needed a home to stay in while they were temporarily homeless. Jon and Jen amaze me with their 'open heart, open house' lifestyle. Many times over their twenty plus years of marriage they have offered warm and wonderful hospitality to others. They have invested in others and God has blessed them for it. They have a host of friends who dearly love them.

But that same thing goes for Cindy and Kermit Bell,

my precious daughter and her dear husband of over thirty-three years of marriage. They, too, amaze me with their generosity, hospitality, and desire to maximize others.

I am sure that they have no idea how many, many times in the past thirty years they have had dinner parties, luncheons, and social gatherings at their home for twenty-five to forty-five people at a time. Big gatherings! I know because Naomi and I have participated in some them.

And the menu is rarely simple. They prepare very tasty meals of smoked salmon on a cedar plank with salads and vegetables; a delicious Cajun boil of fish, shrimp, and crawfish with potatoes and corn on the cob; and tender smoked prime rib with lots of special dishes of fruit and veggies. Sometimes Kermit will serve his special recipe of home-baked chocolate cookies. As I write this my mouth is salivating . . . oh, man, does this all sound delicious!

My children love people! They love to enrich and encourage others! Just ask people who know them and have probably been a participant with them in their homes.

Where did they learn to be so caring, loving and giving? From the most wonderful mother two children could ever have . . . my lovely wife, Naomi! Her example through the years of our being senior pastors first in Houston and then later in Austin taught them that 'maximizing others' is such a joy. Naomi on many occasions would almost single-handedly prepare terrific dinners in our home for all the deacons and their wives plus members of the pastoral team and their marriage partners. There would be other times that we would have dinners in our home for new comers to the church. Many of them became faithful members in the congregation.

When Naomi broke her left femur and endured four surgeries over an eight year period in the 1990's, our lifestyle had to change. Later in 2006 when she began her battle against lymphoma for several years our lives were drastically altered. But by then the example of being a gracious, hospitable hostess was ingrained in our children.

Cindy and Kermit have two beautiful twin daughters, Katie and Sarah, who have carried on the tradition of assisting others. Both of them know how to prepare and provide special events for others. They, too, are great cooks. Their younger brothers, Christopher and Michael, know how to prepare delectable, flavorful salmon smoked on a cedar plank. Wow! So tasty! I'm not sure about the youngest Bell, Joshua, as to his being a gourmet cook, but I do know he loves children and they love him. Investing in others, what a great investment for now and for eternity.

And I must not fail to speak of the wonderful grandchildren in the Schober household; they, too, are developing into teens who know how to host a gathering of their friends and provide lots of good food that they have prepared themselves.

It runs in the family! I'm not sure that it is in their DNA, but I am sure that they have been affected by the environment they have seen in their own home with their mom and dad, and they have also seen in the Bell's home where Aunt Cindy and Uncle Kermit have graciously given of themselves often. What great role models!

Naomi and I became parents just a few days before we celebrated our first anniversary as husband and wife. Cynthia Von discovered America on June 16 and we celebrated our marriage on June 25. Naomi's birthday is June 13, so June is a big month for our family.

Jonathan David, our son, came into our home about ten years after Cindy did. His story is such a 'God-Thing' that I really need to share it with you.

It was at Thanksgiving time in November, 1971, that I was serving as the district youth director for the South Texas District of the Assemblies of God and giving leadership to the annual youth convention which was at the famous Shamrock Hilton Hotel in Houston. Some say there were nearly two thousand in attendance as we enjoyed the music of Andre Crouch and the Disciples who were introduced to Texas at this convention. It started

Wednesday night, continued all day on Thanksgiving Day, and then concluded on the Friday thereafter. It was a very memorable event!

For Naomi, Cindy, and me it was memorable for another reason. On Wednesday evening one of the directors of the Pleasant Hills Children's Home in Fairfield, Texas, came to me with this message: "Vic, we know where there is a perfect little nine month old boy who must be placed in a home with a family who will adopt him . . . it must be done by Sunday or he will become a ward of the state of Texas. You know so many people all across South Texas; do you know anybody who wants to adopt a child?"

My answer was spoken with emotion as I slapped my hand a couple of times against my chest and said: "Yeah, we do!" Naomi and Cindy had been praying earnestly for over two weeks that the Lord would keep our little boy wherever he was. Well, he was in Fairfield and was waiting for us to pick him up!

To make this exciting story a bit shorter it was Sunday morning before we went to church that Naomi and I sat down with Cindy to say: "Honey, we have something wonderful to tell you." Before we could get it out she said: "We're going to get a little boy, aren't we?" We were totally surprised at her question and asked her if she had heard us talking about what we were planning to tell her. She responded: "No, but is that what is about to happen?"

We then said, "Yes, we will pick him up later this afternoon." Cindy burst into tears and put her head down into her mother's lap and cried for joy as she said, "That's all I want for Christmas!" Oh, it was an exciting day!

Later that Sunday afternoon we drove onto the one thousand acre Pleasant Hills Children's Home ranch and met our new son. He indeed was perfect! What a fabulous thing God had orchestrated! Within four days of my hearing about him in Houston, we were gathering together the few clothes that he possessed, loading them and him into our car and driving back to our home off the Gulf Freeway in southeast Houston.

Now there were four in the Vic Schober family. It would be six months later that he legally became a Schober, but unofficially he was ours from the first day we met. It really was a 'God- Thing'!

Little did we know that we were making an investment in a handsome little boy who would bless us later in life with seven terrific grandchildren: John David, Rachel, Kaitlyn, Kristin, Joseph, Jack, and Annalise. What a great dividend is ours from one investment!

Well, that is one of many stories that really blesses me as I look back over the years of investing in others . . . people who would later bless me over and over again!

I could tell you stories about other 'sons' in whom we have invested . . . 'spiritual sons' . . . like James Kermit Bell, our son-in-love. What a powerful preacher/pastor he has become! He has ministered all over the world! But he and Cindy have had many ministry trips to Romania, El Salvador, and Uganda where they have touched the lives of thousands upon thousands of lives. He ministered one New Year's Eve to over 100,000 in Uganda alone.

Kermit and I served together for 18 years on the pastoral staff at GTaustin where he very adequately filled several different positions over the years: business administrator, praise and worship leader, young adult's class teacher, assistant pastor, and then executive pastor. Now I have the joy of serving with him again, only this time he is the senior pastor and I give leadership to the OASIS Ministry (Older Adults Serving, Interacting, Sharing). We both serve together as executive presbyters on the North Texas District Executive Presbytery under the very able leadership of Rick Dubose, our district superintendent for NTD. There are twelve great leaders serving on that EP Board.

There are other 'spiritual sons' like John Collins, Tommy Thompson, and Mark Summers. Each one served with us as youth pastors at GTaustin during the years from 1976 to 2003. And I had some impact, I think, on others like Lee Fruh, Edwin Ennis, and Jesse Martin. These men and their wives also served with us as outstanding youth pastors to the glory of God.

Having been a 'spiritual father' to these and others is such a blessed memory for me. I once remember John Collins telling me just a few months before his untimely death due to a genetic heart problem, he said: "Pastor, have you ever considered that you have many 'spiritual grandsons' due to my ministry as your 'spiritual son'? I've brought many sons and daughters into the Kingdom during my lifetime and it would never have happened if you hadn't brought me to Christ and mentored me along the way." That was really a new thought for me to consider. Then I began to think of all the other ministers who we coached and mentored in Houston and in Austin. Oh, hallelujah! What wonderful, multiplied dividends from our investments into various individual lives. The Scripture says, "Sow abundantly! Reap abundantly!" And I believe it! I've experienced it!

If you are really serious about 'maximizing others' why not consider doing the following things to build greater relationships that will help to boost them:

1. Put others first. "Serve (others) wholeheartedly, as if you were serving the Lord, not men" (Eph. 6:7 NIV). If you take that mindset into all your dealings with others, they will be made stronger and healthier.

2. Invest in your most valuable relationships. Be careful not to give away your most valuable time on a first-come-first-served basis. Don't let the squeaky wheels take so much of your time that you do not have anything left for those who matter most to you. Keep a list of who has priority in your life and give them

your best.

3. Serve others gladly. One airline executive explained how difficult it is to hire and train people for his industry. "Service is the only thing we have to sell, but it's the toughest thing to teach because very few people want to be thought of as a servant." Be like your Lord . . . Be there to serve, not to be served!

4. Constantly express your appreciation. Tell your loved ones how much you love them—and do it often. Too many people think that the best way to help someone is to criticize them or give them 'the benefit of your wisdom.' Wrong! Don't be one of them! Really the best way to maximize others is to see the best in them. Practice the 101 percent principle: Look for one thing to admire; then give them 100 percent encouragement for it!

I want you to hear personally from my son, Jonathan David Schober Sr. He has a really unique story to share about where the Lord has led him thus far. It hasn't always been easy! There have been some 'up' times, for sure; but there have been some 'down' times, too . . . but the Lord has been with him through it all. I know you will be thrilled as you read his story in the next chapter!

Jesus Saves! Moses Invests!

LESSONS LEARNED BY EXPERIENCE

By Jon Schober (Son of Vic Schober)

There are times when introspection is good and having to give an account of one's lifestyle can be productive.

I have recently asked myself a few questions like: (1) how has God worked in my life in this thing of 'saving' and 'investing'? (2) Have I taken advantage of the opportunities that He has given me? (3) Am I becoming the person that God designed me to be? (4) Have I searched like a king would search, for the glory that God has hidden within me as mentioned in Proverbs 25:2? "It is the glory of God to conceal a matter; to search out a matter is the glory of kings."

As I think back over my life I see myself as a twelve-year-old Austinite who wanted to make some money that summer rather than doing the 'typical' thing . . . mowing lawns for neighbors. I was motivated to make money because I wanted to enroll in a series of lessons at Lake Travis that would teach me how to SCUBA dive.

But I had two problems: (1) I hated manual labor and mowing lawns on a hot afternoon under a hot Texas sun just didn't appeal to me. (2) I was pretty sure that my dad didn't want to pay to have our lawn mower repaired due to my possibly breaking it during my mowing venture.

But what could I do to make money? Fortunately my dad shared with me an idea that sounded like fun and it basically didn't require slaving in the summer heat.

He and I would create custom flyers that could be distributed door to door advertising local businesses. Understand that this was before the days of PC and virtual 'cut and paste' abilities. We would go to the yellow page ads and literally cut and paste different looking, newly designed advertising flyers that I could distribute in neighborhoods near these businesses. The most high-tech equipment we had available to us was a Xerox copier.

Dad's idea of developing a small advertising business required me to talk with local businessmen, professional people like dentists and chiropractors, and a few other folks who would want to be known to our community. I became a sales person pitching my desire to work for them and many others like them in developing, printing, and distributing hundreds of flyers on their behalf. To my surprise I found favor with a lot of them.

As it happened we were able to sell this idea to fourteen different business concerns that summer. We printed flyers, collated them, bundled them, and then I distributed them going door to door to hundreds of homes.

I hope that these businessmen gained an ROI for investing in my marketing effort, but as I look back I'm convinced that most of them were simply willing to invest in the next generation. As I recall I made over a thousand dollars that summer.

Presently I am involved with an organization dedicated to 'providing young people with a fundamental understanding of how money works, inspiring them to establish habits that build a life of financial stability and independence.' It's called 'Moolah U' and can be found at www.molahu.com. I have enjoyed helping the next generation just as those fine business people were willing to help me some thirty years ago.

Dad helped me establish another business a couple of summers later that didn't succeed nearly as well as our advertising business. It was a snow cone stand.

For several different reasons, it flopped. I think I ate more snow cones than I sold. But just because the venture wasn't a success didn't mean that the investment wasn't worthwhile. I learned a lot . . . but I'll save sharing about that for another day. I have come to believe that these are not 'failures' but just 'experiments' that provide learning experiences along the way.

Following graduation from high school I pursued several different interests into which I invested my time and energies. I learned great lessons from all of those ventures.

One year I was a volunteer fireman in my community. Another year I enrolled in the Travis County Sheriff's Academy and spent four months in training to be a deputy officer. Although I was never employed either as a fire fighter or a peace officer, I discovered that these became building blocks in my development as a man with many varied experiences. After being a college student for several semesters, I joined the United States Air Force. That, too, was another building block that provided many unique opportunities for development.

All of these ventures eventually led me to twenty years in IT service and marketing. Even my time in IT has been a building block to what I am presently doing as a 'leadership coach.'

Let me share with you about the day that I was fired from a dot com company in Austin.

I had been the IT person for over three years for the Texas Republican Party and I had enjoyed my time there. But when I was approached to join a new company that was developing and I was offered a salary that was really terrific, I decided to 'go for it.'

I was now living the American Dream . . . riding the huge wave of what would become the tech bubble in 2000. It appeared that the sky was the limit.

One day as I had been working for this technological startup company for nine months, it suddenly came to an abrupt end! I went to work as usual. Put my key in the door and discovered that the locks had been changed. I no longer had a job. My services were no longer needed. I was now unemployed!

I'll never forget that it happened on my daughter's birthday. I returned home, walked in the door to our home after being gone for less than an hour, and had to announce to my wife, Jennifer, that I had just been terminated.

So, we began to assess our situation. How would we pay our house mortgage, our car payment, and the payments for a huge student loan? Lots of unanswered questions!

As we talked about these things, suddenly Jennifer remembered that there was a birthday cake in the oven. She rushed over to the kitchen stove, removed the cake, and found that it had not risen properly. It looked like we felt . . . a deflated tire! I'll never forget it!

Out of that tragedy we began to restructure our way of living. We began to learn important lessons from Dave Ramsey's teachings in 'Baby Steps.' It can still be found online at www.daveramsey.com/baby-steps.

He taught us many things:

- Establishing a $1000 Baby Emergency Fund
- Getting out of debt (other than the house payment)
- Ceasing to have a credit card
- Having a 3-6 months of savings in a Full Emergency Fund
- Investing 15% of my salary in a retirement fund
- Seeking to pay off the debt on our home early
- Learning to build wealth by tithing and giving

Soon I was employed by Dell Computers where I worked for the next ten years. During that decade we used what is called 'envelope living.' Check it out at www.daveramsey.com/envelope-system-explained.

After several years and more than $100,000 later, we were completely debt free! It felt GREAT!

But life is full of surprises! After a decade at Dell there came that day when I was asked to join a late afternoon meeting with my immediate supervisor, the HR representative, and the director. I knew what was coming.

At that meeting they told me that Dell was reorganizing and reducing their workforce. They gave me thirty days to find another job at Dell or I would be laid off.

I took the thirty days to look for another job with Dell, but in the end decided that it was time to take the severance package that was offered and move on. But this time it was not nearly as scary as when I had lost my job ten years earlier.

This time we were out of debt. This time we were prepared for the crises. This time we had money available that could carry us through many months of not receiving a monthly paycheck.

Now I could take a sabbatical with my family. I could spend time transitioning to my next chapter in life. I could more easily develop a new venture without overwhelming pressure.

These days when I tell my story I will often say, "I know what it is to be fired and I know what it is to be laid off. Laid off is much better. I know what it is to lose a job before and after Dave Ramsey's teachings. After Dave Ramsey's teachings is much better!"

Presently I am developing a new chapter in my life: I am a personal coach. I teach people how to discover their strengths and understand their core design with my Personal Vision Resources program. I am attempting to 'maximize others through empowerment and encouragement.' Check out my website for more information at www.maximizeothers.com. Obviously I believe in investing in others!

You might want to check out my podcasts: 'Coffee with Jon' and 'The Jon and Joe Show.'

As Dad has said 'Jesus Saves! Jesus Invests!' I also believe it! I, too, want to not only save, but I also want to invest my life in helping others to become all that the Lord wants them to be..

ABOUT THE AUTHOR

VIC SCHOBER is an experienced public speaker and teacher, author, pastor, television and radio presenter, composer, and administrator. He has spent most of his life in Texas fulfilling the call upon his life to follow Christ. He has ministered in more than forty nations of the world and has published four other books including THE (H)IMPOSSIBLE WAY. Vic has made investments throughout his adult lifetime that have given him many experiences that qualify him to share the wisdom that he has acquired. You will be wiser for having read this book!